The Secure Company

The Secure Company

CHARLES F. HEMPHILL, Jr.
Senior Consultant
Loss Prevention Division
Wackenhut Systems Corporation

THOMAS HEMPHILL
Administrative Analyst
City of Downey
Downey, California

1975

54168

Dow Jones-Irwin, Inc.
Homewood, Illinois 60430

First Printing, March 1975

Library of Congress Cataloging in Publication Data
Hemphill, Charles F.
    The secure company.

    1. Personnel management. 2. Employee theft.
3. Retail trade—Security measures. I. Hemphill,
Thomas, joint author. II. Title.
HF5549.H3926   658.3   74-24462
ISBN 0-87094-071-6

Printed in the United States of America

To   To
Phyllis   Julie

Preface

THIS BOOK is about the problems caused by the dishonesty, disloyalty, and disinterest of employees and how these attitudes can be changed or sufficiently controlled so that your company can provide a secure and productive environment for profitable growth.

Employee performance is often a reflection of the basic attitudes of management. Owners or managers of a firm may feel that they have absolute authority over the functions of the business and that therefore they can demand absolute compliance. This may be true from the standpoint of immediate control in specific situations. Over the long run, however, worker performance is inclined to mirror the honesty, loyalty, and interest of the individuals who run the business.

This book is not a deep or technical work, but it can give the manager or supervisor approaches to solving problems of employee behavior that can stand in the way of accomplishing legitimate goals of economical, productive, and profitable operations. The subject matter is approached from both personnel management and loss prevention standpoints. Legal and labor arbitration cases are cited to show contemporary opinions and decisions that have set precedents for action by managers and supervisors in controversial areas involving, for example, the enforcement of company rules regarding theft, chronic absenteeism, and so on. These examples should help to simplify the settlement of disputes and avoid lawsuits.

We are indebted to Ervin Spindel, director of the departments of Community Development and Public Works for the City of Downey, California; D. E. Rynerson, chief engineer of the Combat Systems Office of the Long Beach Naval Shipyard; and George W. Ford, Jr., of Deseret Pharmaceuticals. We also express appreciation to Benjamin C. Butcher, Robert T. Holmes, John R. Stuteville, and Dale Yoder of the Graduate School of Business Administration at California State University, Long Beach. Anita Hemphill provided considerable help in furnishing useful suggestions and in manuscript preparation.

A special thank you goes to Julie Hemphill who, during her first year of marriage, gave up much of her time to become an editor. Without her support and help, this book would remain unfinished. Appreciation also goes to Phyllis Hemphill for her encouragement, manuscript consultations, and past editing.

February 1975   CHARLES F. HEMPHILL, JR.
                              THOMAS HEMPHILL

Contents

section two
Personnel Practices for Prevention and Control

Search. Employee Lockers. Employees Who Work Unsupervised—Janitorial, Temporary, and Maintenance Employees. Curtailing Janitorial Access. Opportunities for Loss. Utilizing Temporary Employees. Construction Workers on the Premises. Management's Responsibility to Protect against Loss.

Management Often Draws a Blank on the Application Blank. Background Checking. Preemployment Testing. Interviewing. Recruiting Employees from Competitors. The Personnel Manual. Assuring Continuity for the Organization. Changes in Employees. Employee Awareness and Loss Prevention Programs.

Closed Circuit TV. Microphones and Videotape Cameras. Recording Phone Conversations. Undercover Workers. Value of the Undercover Operation. The Polygraph as a Tool to Prove Misconduct. Cash Register Irregularities. Use of a Shopping Service to Detect Failure to Record. Taking Action against Employees When Theft Cannot Be Proved.

Management's Approach to Discharge. Records and Forms Regarding Terminations. Discharge for Off-Duty Misconduct. Keeping Lines of Communication Open. Ethics of the Departing Employee. Confidentiality of Customer Lists. Rights to Company Records and Papers. Stealing Customers. Inquiries Regarding Former Employees.

Why Do People Work? Alleviating Boredom. The New Breed of Employee. Women in the Work Force. The Management of Mistakes. Flattery. Disillusionment. Summary.

1

Introduction

CRIMES against business are often brutally physical in execution and immediate in impact. As a consequence, management is increasingly forced to mount massive and costly efforts to protect employees and assets. But the chief anxiety of business is not with these outside losses, serious though they may be. Violent incidents make headlines, but it is the less spectacular noncriminal misconduct of persons inside the company that steadily erodes the profit structure. Loss from this source is directly traceable to employee disinterest, disloyalty, or dishonesty.

These attitudes stem in part from the employee's relationship to management and the degree of his identification with the firm that employs him. The recent proliferation of anticompany acts, self-serving schemes, downright dishonesty, or crime that falls short of violence has threatened to destroy the trust and confidence upon which America's social and economic institutions are founded. At times, as much effort and ingenuity may have to be expended to protect profits from employee manipulations as to earn profits in the first place.

1

This does not mean that the majority of individuals in the work force have been alienated. On the whole, employees are conscientious, honest individuals who have the firm's best interests at heart. Few companies could stay in business very long if this were not so. It is the exception to this rule that concerns us here.

Employee attitudes are also directly affected by personal problems that originate both within the organization and outside it. It is contended by some that management should not interfere in the private lives of employees—that unsolicited counseling is anything but welcome. It is also frequently argued that a business firm is not a psychiatric or medical clinic and has no facilities to rehabilitate problem employees. The argument is that no one in business should be expected to serve as his brother's keeper.

In truth, no subject is of greater concern to any enterprise than the care and well-being of its employees. From the profit standpoint, this is only a matter of common sense. If procedures are not effective in regulating employees, for a certain number of them selfish motives and personal schemes will be allowed to carry over into work assignments. When this happens damage to the profit structure can result. It is therefore management's responsibility to understand the problems deliberately created by employees and to know how to deal with them.

Some of these employee activities may be criminal in nature but not of the type that the firm would want to prosecute. However, they are dishonest by almost any standard. Still other activities may be neither illegal nor dishonest but reflect a complete lack of concern for the company and its property. The end result is the same. Dishonesty, disloyalty, and disinterest are managerial problems that cannot long be ignored if the profit potential is to be maintained.

Anticompany acts may go unnoticed or may cause little impact because some executives tend to view such activities as the concern of society rather than business. They maintain that they have no control over social conditions and that law enforcement agencies should deal with illegal acts. Many of the self-seeking schemes of employees are not within the responsibilities of the police, however. Even when crime is involved, the sole obligation of law enforcement is the apprehension and prosecution of the lawbreaker. Police priorities do not include concern for business loss or why the employee took advantage of his own firm.

Management also is inclined to believe that the recent increases in crime justify the rationalization that theft must be considered as a cost of doing business. It is inconsistent, however, to shrug off a relatively inexpensive theft but become concerned with a major loss. Loss is loss. A manager cannot attempt to negotiate the level at which he will be concerned and below which he will ignore employee misconduct.

While national crime statistics may be on the rise, a private business does not face the same uncontrollable factors as does society. The firm can exercise control over those who have been hired, the physical environment, and the system and procedural controls under which all must operate. There is no valid reason for management to accept losses as "just another cost of doing business."

How Management Can Profit by the Experience of Others

Some of the examples included in this book are legal cases that have been adjudicated by the courts. Others are cases that have been settled by labor arbitration. When employees belong to a labor union, members often utilize the grievance machinery that has been set up in the union contract. In the typical situation of this kind, the employee has already been discharged or suspended and makes the appeal to the labor arbitrator in the hope that he can be reinstated or that the penalty can be reduced in some manner.

There are no absolute managerial guidelines for avoiding the problems created by employees. Neither is there any way a firm can always prevail in the courts or in hearings before arbitration officials. But with planning, management can work out a healthy pattern for decision making in this regard. Much of the material presented here has been designed for use in setting up procedures to avoid costly and time-consuming disputes, hearings, and lawsuits. Employee controversy almost always means business cost.

This material may help management and supervisors to anticipate some of the problems that can arise by discussing the experiences of others. In a number of instances, actual case histories are examined. The results reached by the courts and by arbitration officials may be disturbing, but they also indicate what can happen in actual situations.

The Right to Manage

A firm's basic obligation to stockholders, to the community, and to employees is to operate at a profit. All activities should be directed toward turning out products and services in the most efficient way that is consistent with good business practices.

This means that the "right to manage" must remain in the hands of those with responsibility to run the company. If management were put in the position where it had to give up this authority, achievement of the profit goal would be almost impossible. While concern for employees is essential, this does not call for relinquishing the decision-making responsibility. Unions may specify that workers have a voice in approving work conditions and methods, but other than such restriction by union contract, it is management that sets organizational goals, controls operations, and sets quality standards.

Management should never be expected to tolerate unsatisfactory work or improper employee behavior. The company is entitled to establish rules of conduct that are not in conflict with the bargaining agreement and to insist on discipline for just cause.

As a case in point, a North Carolina cotton mill firm was forced to absorb a loss because of the great number of seconds being produced by weavers at this mill. To correct this situation, management set up a penalty for production of seconds in excess of 15 percent of the worker's output. The punishment for the first offense was a warning; after the sixth violation, the employee was discharged.

These penalties were in addition to a long-standing rule providing for the loss of half of one's pay for any worker who produced seconds in excess of 10 percent of his production for the week. The union that represented the weavers objected to these additional penalties. When the case came up for arbitration, it was pointed out that there was no provision to the contrary in the contract between the union and the company. Accordingly, the arbitrator held that the company had the right to manage, and that this included the setting of quotas and quality standards. As an extension of this right, it was held that management could penalize employees who failed to meet these requirements. The arbitrator pointed out that the standards were not capricious and that the penalty had a logical relationship to the employee failure.

The Right to Protect Private Property

It is well established in our system of free enterprise that a plant, factory, or business is private property. Management has the right to authorize necessary security or regulatory measures to protect this property.

In one recent case, a plant manager made a decision to permanently close one of the automobile gates giving access to the employee parking lot. This gate had been open to employees for a number of years, but it was found that the gate also frequently gave entry to drifters, peddlers, and car thieves. It was difficult to maintain good security in the parking lot as long as this gate remained opened.

Union representatives at the firm complained that management had no right to close the gate because doing so caused inconvenience to some employees entering the plant. When the union insisted on making an issue of this matter, the arbitrator held that management was within its rights to maintain the gate in a closed condition. It had the right to control its own property in a reasonable manner in order to protect the property and to protect employees' cars in the parking lot.

Providing a Climate of Honesty

Every effort should be made to maintain a climate of honesty within the work organization. Management can set an example by protecting and conserving all assets of the company, no matter how little value may be involved. Company officials also have the opportunity and the responsibility of guiding employee activities by the attitudes they create. Because employee thinking is often influenced by management activities that filter down to rank-and-file workers, every effort should be made to be honest and fair in all dealings with employees, customers, and stockholders.

If the executive policy is to disregard local fire and safety regulations, to deliberately cheat on income tax provisions, or to operate outside state and local laws, it should not come as a surprise if employees fail to adhere to a policy of strict honesty in their own activities. Using "executive privilege" as an excuse for disregarding a company security rule is at most a questionable practice. Employees also make judgments from the firm's attitudes toward customer relations. If company officials exhibit a calloused attitude in this regard or underbid a contract with the intent of supplying inferior materials, lack of respect from employees can be expected.

No firm can anticipate that there will be blind compliance with every desire of management. But basic honesty, loyalty, and job interest should be expected from all employees. Dishonest employee behavior, whether it is termed criminal or merely unethical, is almost always translated into cash loss for the business. This frequently results in increased prices to the customer, reducing the flexibility of the business to compete in an open market. Disloyal behavior can endanger the firm's competitive position. And disinterested behavior can eat away at productivity and morale until it seriously endangers profit potential and organizational effectiveness.

Management Control through Employee Attitudes

Management's job in controlling employee behavior consists of getting things done through others. Ideally, it inspires interest and enthusiasm so that employees themselves will want to accomplish the things management is seeking to achieve. Unless management expresses feeling for employee problems, there may be no end to anticompany acts. Company leadership achieves its goals through awareness of human problems and sensitivity toward the aspirations and hopes of employees, coupled with a capacity for analysis of the needs and desires that motivate their conduct.

Thus management can guide the work force most effectively by making certain that company rules of conduct have been formulated and brought to the attention of all employees. Each individual then should understand what is expected of him. When an employee deliberately violates the rules, a determination can be made as to the reasons behind this action and steps can be taken to remedy the situation.

The dishonest, disloyal, and disinterested behavior discussed here, along with suggestions on how management can control or prevent it, have been divided into two main categories: (1) evidences of employee misconduct and (2) personnel practices designed to forestall such acts by rules and regulations. The first deals primarily with specific acts by employees that adversely affect job performance. The second suggests procedures in personnel management which can help in preventing or coping with such problems. The two sections are not mutually exclusive, but the major argument of the chapters in each one is directed to these topics.

The final chapter provides insight into the idea that management itself may be responsible for the alienation of employees and suggests a positive program of career development as a remedy.

EVIDENCES OF EMPLOYEE MISCONDUCT

2

Drugs in the Work Environment

UNTIL recent years, the problem of drug abuse was of little concern to business. As a social problem, it troubled only law enforcement and health authorities. Most members of management had little exposure to the problem, in either their work or social relationships. As people of all ages and lifestyles have "turned on" to drugs in increasing numbers, however, it has become apparent that the problem has invaded both the businessman's home and his place of work.

The business community has much to learn in getting this problem under control. This is due, in part, to the fact that many drug users are not readily distinguishable from other individuals. They are alike only in that they believe that drugs can give them understanding, peace, wisdom, or the ability to attain their fullest potentials.

A major Connecticut firm recently gave notice of its involvement with the drug problem by stating that the company had "grown up" in that community and therefore had an obligation to the people of the area. It announced that as a proposed solution it would voluntarily hire and work with local drug users.

11

Such a policy undoubtedly originated with a sense of civic responsibility and should prove of value for the community. However, it could also prove to be costly to the firm from a profit and loss standpoint. Business and industrial losses related to drug usage include increased merchandise pilferage, high employee turnover, excessive absenteeism, poor work performance, and an increased number of accidents on the job. Higher insurance rates naturally follow. There may also be an increase in taxes to support the mental health, police, and medical facilities needed to service drug abusers.

Drug users are rarely caught in the act at work. When they are fired, it is usually not because they have been observed "mainlining" into a vein or pill popping. Rather, dismissal is ordinarily due to the side effects of the drugs, which can take the form of falling asleep on the production line, perpetual tardiness, absenteeism, or failure to meet quotas. Company thefts can be motivated by the user's need to finance his habit. Of course, all of these create higher operational overhead.

Industrial espionage can even enter the picture. Employees in sensitive positions have been known to turn over trade secrets to competitors as blackmail payoff when their drug usage has been discovered by undercover operatives of rival firms. Even vandalism and outright sabotage of plant equipment and buildings have been attributed to "spaced-out" drug users.

Extent of Employee Involvement

The extent of drug use by employees has been indicated by a number of recent surveys and reports. A year-long survey of drug usage among employees was completed by the New York State Narcotics Addiction Control Commission in July 1971. This study was based on detailed results of interviews with 7,500 typical employees from all levels of the work force and from all areas of the state. The New York State research pointed out that there was widespread usage among workers of a number of drugs, both legal and illegal, from barbituates to marijuana, morphine, and heroin. In addition, these researchers reported, drugs were often taken on the job, apparently to enable the users to face up to the daily stresses they encountered.

One study done in the early 1970s detailed numerous cases of illegal drug consumption in organizations, irrespective of number of employees, kind of business, or size of operation.[1] Observers of the American drug scene indicate that the number of people turning to drugs will be increasing for some time. The hard drug problem is even now widespread enough for the U.S. Bureau of Narcotics and Dangerous Drugs to warn that any employer with 50 or more workers can expect to have drug users among its ranks.

A comprehensive survey of drug use among applicants tested for business clients was completed in September 1972 by the Wackenhut Corporation, a leading firm in investigating the background and qualifications of job applicants.[2] A sample of 4,000 individuals with drug experience was selected, and interviews were conducted during a six-month span. In this random sample, the frequency of drug usage was broken down as follows:

Experimentally (one to five times) 32%
Occasionally (up to once every two weeks) 17
Regularly (at least once a week up to daily). 51

One third of the same group had discontinued use of drugs, while the remainder continued to use them on an occasional or regular basis.

Of drug users sampled, 100 percent had started with marijuana. Those who graduated to other drugs frequently continued use

[1] National Clearinghouse for Drug Abuse Information, "Drug Abuse in Industry," Selected Reference Series 6, No. 1 (Rockville, Md., July 1973), p. 1; "Firms Seem Reluctant to Give Drug Tests," *Industry Week,* July 24, 1972, p. 27.

[2] *Pipeline,* Vol. 8, No. 3 (September 1972). Details reprinted by permission of the Wackenhut Corporation, Coral Gables, Florida.

of marijuana on a regular basis. This created an overlapping of percentages in the types of drugs used, which were as follows:

Marijuana 62%
Soft drugs (amphetamines, barbiturates, hallucinogens) 33
Hard drugs (heroin, morphine, codeine) 10

Thus while not all individuals who had experimented with marijuana went on to hard drugs, all heavy drug users in the study began with it. From pot smoking, 33 percent began using such dangerous drugs as amphetamines (stimulants), barbiturates (sedatives), and hallucinogens like LSD (lysergic acid diethylamide). Ten percent had histories of addiction to hard drugs such as heroin, morphine, and codeine.

Other details of the study show how critical the drug problem is and indicate the present high probability that a firm will employ drug users.

One surprising fact that emerges from these studies and reports is that the fastest growth rate of hard drug users appears to be among young middle-class white females, ages 15 to 23—not the ghetto-born shoplifter, as is usually presumed.[3]

Robert W. Goldfarb, who has had considerable experience in working with drug users, has pointed out that most heroin addicts do not work, but "keeping high is a seven-day-a-week job." Those who do work usually are retail clerks, but, he notes:

No addict will work for you if he can't steal from you. . . . Weeding out drug users from your job applicants and employees is no easy task. In the morning, an addict is indiscernible from normal employees because he has just had a fix. But by noon he begins to look ill and, to make his connection, he has already stolen from your stock. Beware the clerk who has failed in his morning attempt—he will be desperate for anything saleable by afternoon.[4]

---

[3] From remarks by Robert W. Goldfarb, president of Urban Directions, Inc. in "Loss Prevention in Broadway and Bullocks," *Stores Magazine*, May 1973, p. 10. © 1973, National Retail Merchants Association.

[4] Ibid.

Detecting Drug Users Among Applicants and Employees

There is no known way for personnel interviewers to detect drug users with complete accuracy. Police departments and narcotics bureaus in some areas can supply brief training sessions or films telling what to look for. The puffy, veinless hands of women may be a telltale sign, and some men use homemade tattoo marks to hide the punctures of hypodermic needles.

The following suggestions are helpful for prescreening applicants or evaluating employees as regards drug usage:

1. Review employment application forms and, if necessary, incorporate questions specifically aimed at detection of drug use. Pay particular attention to what are termed soft drugs: marijuana, amphetamines, barbiturates, and hallucinogenics.
2. Survey present preemployment screening procedures and incorporate steps aimed specifically at detecting drug users. Users may admit taking drugs on an experimental basis, but they will not volunteer information on habitual drug taking. Background investigations are excellent tools. The application of preemployment polygraph testing, where legally allowed, is highly recommended.
3. Establish training programs for personnel staffs to acquaint them with the drugs and their physical and mental effects. This includes learning the drug vocabulary.
4. Hold management conferences and draw firm guidelines for dealing with drug users who are employee applicants, as well as for present employees who become drug users.
5. Ask local narcotics officials for additional suggestions.

While urine chromatography tests for narcotic abuse can be given, sometimes careful observation can be used instead. Sleepiness, running eyelids, flushing of the face, depression, stuttering, constant scratching, confusion, and pinpoint eye pupils can indicate drug use in people. Detection is complicated because some drugs are "uppers" while others are "downers"; some lead to hyperactivity and others to apathy. Also, individuals may have different reactions to the same drug.

When interviewing applicants or evaluating current employees, it is important to be aware that a noticeable decline in many men's and women's job performance can be caused by narcotics. It is wise to be cautious about placing such personnel in areas that are highly susceptible to theft. Those who have constant sickness or tardiness records for poor reasons, who need advances on their paychecks, or who are often in unassigned areas are open to question.

While management is generally in agreement that eliminating a drug-abusing applicant is more feasible than having to cope with the same person as an employee, it is often hesitant in instituting comprehensive chemical screening programs for applicants and current workers. Workers have been known to view such programs as evidence of bad faith, especially for long-standing, loyal employees. Further, not all laboratory tests are fully accurate for detection purposes.

Action When an Employee Is Found Using Drugs

When an employee is discovered using drugs or is known to be in possession of them, two immediate decisions must be made. The decision to notify police authorities should never be open to question, because failure to notify authorities represents complete abandonment of responsibility to the business and to other employees. The available facts indicate that the retention of an addict on the payroll increases the probability of serious accidents and repeated acts of theft, as well as the possibility that other employees may also become addicted.

The decision to physically take drugs from a user could be questionable, however. He may be "high" at the time and could resort to violent action to protect his drug supply.

After an employee has been arrested for drug usage or possession, the next decision is whether he should be continued as an employee while awaiting trial or while on probation. Some firms discharge an employee outright in a situation of this kind, feeling that they must look beyond the personal emotions and situations of employees in deciding what is good for the business. Any member of management expects to make impersonal, dollars and cents, profit and loss decisions. Business economy is oriented toward performance and results, and the penalty for failure is oblivion. No firm should be saddled with the risks that accompany continuing drug usage.

Nevertheless, from a humanitarian approach as well as that of practical business, it may be preferable to retain an employee who seems to be sincere in agreeing to submit to control. It might seem simplest to recommend the immediate discharge of all employees who are discovered to have such problems as drug usage or alcoholic overconsumption. In the present-day world, however, there is no certainty that the employee's replacement will not himself turn out to be a drug user or an alcoholic. The training of a replacement is costly and time-consuming. When turnover of key personnel is high, it automatically follows that on-the-job experience is low. And in the competitive world of business, a firm may rise or fall on the decisions made on the basis of work experience.

Businessmen have traditionally expressed the idea that people are a firm's most important asset. This truism has become more apparent as techniques for human resource accounting have become more exacting. In terms of money, good employees are hard to replace. The more obvious costs involved in making an employee productive include advertising, interviewing, screening, training, and orientation. An employee is even more of a burden to replace if he or she has supervisory or executive responsibility.

Therefore, it may be preferable to salvage an employee when there is a reasonable chance of success at rehabilitation, rather than to issue a discharge for a drug problem. Unless the worker is willing to acknowledge the problem and to seek help, however, it may be desirable to terminate him at the earliest possible time. There can be no definite answers in situations of this kind.

Management is not an end in itself in any of its aspects. It seeks to obtain a satisfactory return from the investment in employee training, but only insofar as this does not subject the firm or other workers to more serious risks.

Legal Problems

Legal difficulties can impede a program requiring chemical tests and physical examinations for narcotic or barbiturate use. Unless an applicant or current employee is caught red-handed, it is often advisable not to state that he is a drug user. Instead of making such a charge, it is best to refer to the side effects of drugs on the person's behavior: disorientation, lethargy, and so forth. In this way, slander suits and civil rights actions can be avoided.

One acceptable way to use such a test is to have the individual voluntarily agree to take it. Refusal to do so, which may seem suspicious, cannot be held against him, however. Before the test is administered, the applicant or worker should sign a written release holding the employer harmless from recourse.

Often overlooked is the organization's duty to the public in detecting and controlling drug usage. Many types of legal difficulties can stem from having a drug user on the payroll. Some of these potential problems are major constitutional questions of freedom. The company could also be held responsible for violations of criminal and drug laws, along with the user, or open to product liability actions or questions of negligence or malpractice. Invasion of privacy and the propriety of agent-principal duties are other areas of concern. It is a function of the legal staff to apprise management of the risks involved in retaining or hiring drug abusers.

Prevention

The merits of stopping a problem before it starts are obvious. One way to do this with the drug problem is to stress its illegality. The major distinction of employee dysfunction due to drugs as opposed to alcohol is that possession of the former is illegal, whereas that is seldom the case with alcohol.

Adequate security of the plant or office is needed, especially in large operations, to guarantee that drugs are not brought to work or used there. Security alone will often discourage those who are curious about narcotics. Drug use should be clearly forbidden in the employee manual.

Remember, however, that for some employees too much publicity about drugs may lead to dabblers' experiments just to find out what the front office is cautioning employees about. For other employees, information about the subject can be a viable prevention tool. One person goes to narcotics and another does not.

Because the reasons which might cause an employee to turn on to drugs often are found in the home, employer-sponsored social get-togethers designed to improve morale and prevent such problems can be more helpful if they include the workers' families. Company literature aimed at solving such off-the-job problems is also useful.

Rehabilitation

Is it possible to turn a drug addict into a profitable employee? Most authorities agree that only a small fraction of confirmed addicts are ever rehabilitated. Few are ever able to completely discard drugs or to use nonnarcotic chemical substitutes.[5]

Nevertheless, the Bell Telephone Company, General Motors, Piney Bowles, Equitable Life of New York, the Kemper Insurance Group, and other firms have initiated efforts aimed at rehabilitating and employing addicts, with documented success.[6] While not all addicts can be returned to useful jobs, some do make the grade. The drug abuser is given professional help through the employer's rehabilitation program. He also is given the self-esteem that comes from having a job.

In such programs the addict may be discharged or laid off for health reasons and given a promise of reinstatement upon complete recovery. The time away from the job is usually about one year, during which the user must be actively enrolled in a genuine rehabilitation program. He is not allowed to go it alone, and the employer makes counselors available for his guidance.[7]

Illinois and Minnesota recently passed laws to mandate health insurance for alcoholism and drug abuse treatment, and it is expected that other states will adopt similar legislation. Such laws indicate to employers that these situations must be handled like other sicknesses.[8]

Once the rehabilitated worker is back in the labor force, it may be a good idea to test his urine for evidence of drug use on an unscheduled basis. This would be a condition of employment for an employee with any serious disease. The firm should also stay in touch with the patient's therapist.

---

[5] Anthony J. Miraval, "Skyscraper Protection," *Security Management*, May 1973, pp. 8–14.

[6] G. P. Bisgeier, "A Medical Department's Experience in Hiring 'Hard Core' Unemployed," *American Journal of Public Health*, August 1969, pp. 1361–65.

[7] Harold M. F. Rush, "When a Company Counsels the Drug Abuser," *Conference Board Record*, May 1972, pp. 11–15.

[8] "Laws Make Alcoholic, Addict Care Mandatory: Employers up Benefits," *Business Insurance*, December 3, 1973, p. 51.

Some industry rehabilitation programs designed to return addicts to conscientious, responsible employment have failed, either because of the high costs incurred or because the human causes of drug abuse were glossed over. Other programs have had success because they were tied in with the rehabilitation programs of other companies and the community. Community resources for drug treatment available throughout the United States are detailed in a directory published by the National Clearinghouse for Drug Abuse Information.[9] A sample page is shown in Figure 1.

Success in rehabilitation is more likely when the behavioral aspects of the situation are considered. Help on the home and family level, where the cause for drug abuse may have started or been nurtured, is particularly effective. One of the most helpful things the employer can do is to promise the return to a good job if there is successful recovery. Without such support, the chances are that the addiction will begin again when the drug abuser's evaluation of himself hits a low point and he returns to the street.

Can a Drug Addict Be Fired When Discovered?

The practicality of retaining a rehabilitated drug user has been viewed; however, there may be cases where management prefers to dismiss narcotics or drug users. In one case an office worker was arrested by the local police when he attempted to obtain cocaine fraudulently from a neighborhood pharmacist. The arrest was duly noted in the local newspaper, and the accused man was given a short sentence in jail after a plea of guilty. Upon returning to his place of employment, he found that he had been discharged. He appealed to arbitration through representatives of his local union.

---

[9] National Clearinghouse for Drug Abuse Information, *National Directory: Drug Abuse Treatment Programs, 1972* (Program Information Services, 5600 Fishers Lane, Rockville, Md., 20852).

FIGURE 1

Example of Page from the National Clearinghouse for Drug Abuse Information's *National Directory: Drug Abuse Treatment Programs, 1972.*

NATIONAL DIRECTORY OF DRUG ABUSE TREATMENT PROGRAMS   CALIFORNIA

Diogenes House
418 Second Street
Davis, California 95616
(916) 756-5665

R. Wayne Harrison
Director

TYPE OF PROGRAM–Outpatient and crisis center, established May 1969. Funds from California Council on Criminal Justice and donations. Services free, offered from converted residence. Drug abusers make up about 40 percent of clientele. (101-150)

SERVICES–Group and family counseling, encounter groups, other group interaction, referral. Also available: crisis intervention, meditation and awareness, educational counseling, job placement, legal intervention, medical-surgical treatment, social services, sensitivity groups.

ADMISSION–No requirements.

CLIENTELE–Abusers of non-narcotics, primarily barbiturates, hallucinogens, and marihuana. Ages range from under 12 to 32 with majority between 13 and 20. Most are white, unemployed students. Blacks, Orientals, and Mexican Americans included among clientele, as are unskilled and semiskilled workers.

STAFF–Full time: 3 counselors, program administrator, business administrator. Part time: 10 counselors, researcher. Volunteers, part time: physician, R.N., 9 counselors, 5 instructors, pharmacist. Former drug abusers: 4 full-time counselors. Budgeted vacancies: 6 counselors, researcher, program administrator, business administrator.

Downey Counseling Center
10818 New Street
Downey, California 90241
(213) 923-9801

Judge Leon Emerson
Acting Director

TYPE OF PROGRAM–A private, nonprofit organization providing psychological counseling on an outpatient basis in space donated by local churches. The program, in operation since September 1969, obtains its funds from donations, 15 percent, and variable patient fees, 85 percent. (36-50)

SERVICES–Referral, family and group counseling, individual psychotherapy, crisis intervention.

Others: encounter and sensitivity or self-awareness groups.

ADMISSION–Preference is given to residents of the southeastern sector of Los Angeles County.

CLIENTELE–Whites outnumber blacks and Mexican Americans. All ages are represented, but persons 17-24 are predominant. Substance abuse includes barbiturates, marihuana, and tranquilizers, but amphetamines and hallucinogens are the most common.

STAFF–Volunteers, part time: 2 psychiatrists, physician, 8 psychologists, 33 counselors, 2 program administrators, 2 business administrators. Former drug abusers: 12 volunteer part-time counselors.

Duarte Self Help Center
1434 East Huntington Drive
Duarte, California 91010
(213) 357-3241, 357-3242

Saif R. Ullah, Director

TYPE OF PROGRAM–Community-based outpatient and crisis center operating from converted office. Emphasis on free drug treatment but also functions in drug abuse prevention. Program research scheduled for completion by October 1971. Financial support from California Council on Criminal Justice, City of Duarte, local school-district, and in-kind donations. Opened February 1971 as result of community efforts begun in 1969. (50-75)

SERVICES–Crisis intervention; family, group, and individual counseling; sensitivity or self-awareness groups. Others available: educational counseling, encounter groups, other group interaction, recreational therapy, job placement, legal intervention, referral.

ADMISSION–No requirements. Medical emergencies are referred to other facilities.

CLIENTELE–Predominantly students, Jewish, users of amphetamines, barbiturates, hallucinogens, heroin. Most are between 13 and 24, although older clients represented. Whites in majority, followed by Mexican Americans, blacks, and Orientals.

STAFF–Full time: psychologist (also serves as director), counselor. Part time: caseworker, R.N., researcher. Volunteers, part time: psychiatrist, physician, paramedic, 2 lawyers, 2 financial advisors, 9 counselors. Former drug abuser, part time: volunteer counselor.

The arbitrator ruled that the discharge was proper and that the company was not required to retain the services of a known cocaine user. It was pointed out that a cocaine addict may develop illusions and hallucinations or attack those around him without provocation. Thus, the arbitrator noted, the user was more likely to cause accidents or serious disruptions in office procedures.[10]

In another recent incident, the police arrested an employee of a large industrial plant on a tip that he was in possession of unprescribed drugs. He was found to have one amphetamine pill and charged with possession of an illegal drug. Eventually the prosecutor dismissed the charge and the worker returned to his job, but he learned that he had been fired for his alleged drug activity. Protesting that he was not a narcotic user, the worker asked for reinstatement.

The arbitrator held that the man was in possession of only one amphetamine tablet and that he had apparently not intended to sell it or other drugs. Under the circumstances, the arbitrator said that this was not the type of conduct an employee would reasonably expect to result in his discharge. The arbitrator reinstated the worker but without back pay, because, he said, the worker knew he was engaged in illegal conduct and the company should not be expected to make good on his back pay.[11]

Another factor apparently considered by this arbitrator was that company rules did not prohibit the possession or misuse of drugs. A definite rule, brought to the attention of all employees, would be helpful in this regard.

---

[10] In re *Chicago Pneumatic Tool Company* (Franklin, Pa.) and *International Association of Machinists*, District No. 83, Local No. 335, AAA Case No. PIT–L–56–61, 38–10, August 8, 1961.

[11] In re *Southwestern Bell Telephone Company* (Houston, Texas) and *Communications Workers of America*, AAA Case No. 71–30–0049–72, September 20, 1972, 59 LA 709.

3

Alcohol's Effect on Business

THE NATIONAL COUNCIL ON ALCOHOLISM has found that $8 billion in damage to business annually results from the four and one-half million employees who overindulge in drinking.[1] Although the business losses from drug abuse are dramatized in the press, they are not reported to have reached this level. Both the American Medical Association and the World Health Organization classify alcoholism as a disease.

Many costly aspects of poor performance can be due to alcoholism: accidents, poor decisions, excessive benefits paid for sick leave, scheduling and production delays, damaged customer relations, and fights on the job are a few. The adverse effects of alcoholism are generally recognized by both unions and management.

Some alcoholics are crafty enough to remain on the job for

---

[1] Stephen Habbe, "Controlling the Alcohol Problem: Not by Management Alone," *The Conference Board Record*, April 1973, p. 31; Marion Sadler and James F. Horst, "Company/Union Programs for Alcoholics," *Harvard Business Review*, September–October 1972, p. 22.

as long as 14 years before detection.[2] It is not just the unemployed skid row derelict who is the problem drinker. Only 3 percent of all alcoholics are out of work, and about half of the alcoholic population has attended college at one time or another. Approximately three quarters of all alcohol abusers are managers or professionals or hold other white-collar jobs.

No matter how devious, the subterfuge of the drinker is sooner or later detected, at least by fellow employees. They may make pointed remarks about his absenteeism or poor output, or inadvertently harm the alcoholic through their good intentions in providing him with a cover-up. If untrained workers or supervisors try to counsel the drinker, it usually ends up as a waste of the Good Samaritan's time.

Upon learning of an alcoholic employee, many managers still react with dismissal. By this kind of action a manager can dodge the problem, saying that his firm does not have any trouble with alcoholics because they are immediately terminated. Such swift separation of the alcoholic may not be the best policy, however. The decision should be examined in the light of two facts:

1. Labor arbitration decisions have recently established parameters for the procedure.
2. Training a new employee may be more costly than rehabilitating the current worker.

Recent Labor Arbitration Decisions

A discharge on grounds of reporting for work intoxicated can usually be sustained if it is contested and goes to arbitration. If possible, the employee's drunken state should be verified by a

---

[2] Larry Lane, "Significant Savings by Business Linked to Early Aid for Alcoholics," *Los Angeles Times,* October 4, 1973, Sec. 1, p. 10. © 1973, Los Angeles Times. Reprinted by permission.

number of independent witnesses. Supervision and management should take a unified stand in a situation of this kind.

In one recent case, it was apparent to the foreman on duty that an employee had come to work drunk. The foreman immediately told the employee that he was not in fit condition for work, but he reported the man as "sick." When management learned the facts a short time later, it terminated the intoxicated worker on the grounds that the safety of his fellow employees could be placed in jeopardy if he were allowed to work. When an appeal was made to arbitration, it was ruled that the employee could have his job back, without being paid for the time off and with loss of seniority. This seems somewhat puzzling, as the worker was clearly drunk. But management's case was hurt considerably because the foreman described the employee as "sick" rather than as "drunk."

There are a good many cases on record in which management endeavored to dismiss an employee who was caught bringing an intoxicant into a plant or business facility. In some of these cases the businesses had always enforced a rule requiring discharge for drinking on the job. Other instances involved situations where a company official took the liquor away from the employee at the plant entrance. In situations of this kind, labor arbitrators have usually held that firing was too extreme a penalty unless the employee had already consumed an appreciable amount of the intoxicant. The difference seems to be the way in which the company rule is worded. If the act of bringing liquor on the premises is a dischargeable offense, the company rules should so state.

Rehabilitation of the Alcoholic

Because alcoholism is classified as a disease, there is some hope for a cure. Yet today, few firms are actively involved in alcohol detection and control, much less in rehabilitation programs. Often managers feel that hospitals, governmental agencies, and charitable institutions supported by the firm should take this responsibility. The poor image of the firm or of its product that might emerge from publicity about a company-sponsored alcoholic rehabilitation program is often cited as a reason for avoiding it. And there are still a number of managers who persist in the idea that employees' personal problems are left at home and do not affect worker performance. Besides, they ask, "Isn't that what Alcoholics Anonymous is for?"

Costs and profits are terms that are understood by all managers. One knowledgeable authority has asserted that for each alcoholic employee who is treated early, the employer can save up to $5,000 in otherwise misspent time and labor costs.[3] When employers in an area band together to fight this problem, the tax burden should decrease as there is less need for city, county, and state programs supported by corporate taxes.

Several firms have reported progress in combating the abuse of drinking by employees. While 100 percent success in a program of this kind is simply not possible with present techniques, some firms report that 60 to 70 percent of all employees seeking help are being successfully rehabilitated. When compared to the poorer recovery figures for the three other major diseases which result in employees losing time from work—heart disease, cancer, and mental illness—company return on investment through the implementation of adequate alcohol treatment programs seems to be paying off very well.

Supervisors' Responsibilities in the Program

When a supervisor notes that an employee's performance is dropping off in either quality or quantity, he should not attempt to diagnose or solve the problem on his own. Only the substandard

---

[3] Lane, "Significant Savings," p. 10.

work itself should be discussed with the individual. If alcoholism seems to be the likely cause of the problem, the supervisor must make the employee aware of the provisions of the company's rehabilitation program for alcoholics, stressing that the worker may be fired unless his performance improves and he voluntarily enlists in the program. This discussion should be held in a face-to-face situation and later summarized in a memo signed by both the supervisor and the employee. Here the latter acknowledges receipt of the ultimatum.

The supervisor should notify management of the warning to the employee by forwarding a copy of the memo to management. A clear statement should be included that the supervisor has requested the employee to sign up for the rehabilitation program in order to seek a recovery from this disease, which decreases his usefulness to the company.

Aside from checking up on the worker's performance on the job while he is not actually in therapy, the supervisor's involvement in the program should end there. Management should, however, be periodically informed of any work improvements observed by the line supervisor during this period. It should be emphasized that the supervisor is only to be trained in understanding, detecting, and monitoring the alcoholic on the job. His role is not meant to include counseling.

At this point it may be wise for management to seek the aid of the drinker's personal physician. The dual support provided at work by the company and on the home front by the family doctor may be the necessary motivator for the employee's rehabilitation.

Employees' Responsibility to Enter the Program

Should an alcoholic worker chose to go "cold turkey" and attempt to quit drinking without utilizing the company treatment, and should he succeed, his job should be restored, possibly even without lost seniority. Such cases of self-cure are rare, but upon verification they should be rewarded. The apparent success of some outside recovery programs should be questioned, however. It is a fact that the best program for help is often the employer-sponsored one, because job security is the major impetus. On-the-job indicators of performance are not available in outside programs.

For the employee who blatantly ignores his supervisor's verbal and written orders to seek recovery, discharge can be justified. Management can show that the employee has signed and acknowledged an order directing him to rehabilitate himself or lose his job. Dismissal can be justified by showing that the employee still abuses himself and his co-workers through continued alcoholic consumption which jeopardizes everyone's safety and his department's output.

One alternative is to suspend the alcoholic for a two-week period if he seems to regard the written and verbal orders to reform as halfhearted. The sobering effect of going without a paycheck for even this short period can create a shocking impact, especially when the employee ordinarily uses a good part of his earnings to support his drinking.

Management's Responsibility for the Program

At the outset management should view the alcoholic as being truly ill, not as a debauched libertine or a mental weakling. This attitude should be passed on from top management to all supervisors. The promise should be made and kept that those who volunteer for rehabilitation will be free of the threat of punishment. Who would join the program voluntarily if exposure could cost them their jobs?

Sessions for all employees to alert them to the devastating

effects of alcohol abuse can be an effective preventative. The need for early exposure of the problem drinker cannot be overstressed. Discovery that a long-trusted employee is a serious alcoholic results in more costly rehabilitation efforts, with less possibility for success.

The experts in rehabilitation can be located in the organization's medical department. Medicine is going more deeply into this problem, constantly gaining added knowledge about causes and cures. If the firm has no medical department and relies on outside services for preemployment physicals and treatment of job-related accidents, the personnel department should be assigned the responsibility of implementing the rehabilitation program, perhaps in conjunction with an outside clinic. One way to do this is to provide coverage for rehabilitation of alcoholism under the firm's group insurance.

Even with a medical department, personnel is the best area for counselors to be placed as a staff function. Staff resources in the personnel department could be reviewed to see whether a current employee can be assigned to handle counseling while the program is under development.

The primary task of the counselor is to get the alcoholic to admit he is in trouble. Such an admission is the first step enrollees must make. Commitment to take action to remedy the situation can be inspired by the counselor's assurance that he is as interested as the employee is in seeing him return to normal. The counselor should be thoroughly trained to point out the alcoholic's shortcomings without slandering him and thereby leaving the firm open to litigation. After the employee has been taken through these steps, he should be put in contact with a professional clinic or the staff physician.

Follow-up is another important consideration in management's responsibility to the program. The counselor and the professional therapist or physician should constantly be in touch with each other in order to determine when the employee can be returned to the job if his situation warranted a temporary suspension, or when he has satisfactorily recovered and can be separated from the treatment program.

Co-workers may resent any seemingly preferential treatment given to a fellow employee undergoing rehabilitation. When such undercurrents are observed, the counselor is in a good position to step in and recommend that the detoxified worker be transferred to another section to avoid conflicts. Once the recovered alcoholic is fully reinstated the counselor need be the only one aware of the earlier problem, unless he feels this knowledge could be of value to the worker's new supervisor.

Further help in setting up a viable program can be obtained by consulting local Alcoholics Anonymous chapters and the National Council on Alcoholism.

Union Involvement

One of the major reasons why some alcoholic rehabilitation programs have failed is because union participation was not encouraged from the beginning. Union members are generally supportive of alcoholic rehabilitation programs when they learn of the drinkers' drain on productivity. Increased productivity is often the basis used by the unions in seeking improved salaries, benefits, and working conditions. When productivity remains constant or falls, there is little justification for management to ratify any increases sought by the union.

Once the program is in its design stage, it is wise to advise employees through house organs and postings on the bulletin boards that the rehabilitation effort will be labor-management sponsored. It also would be a good plan to encourage similar statements in union newsletters. Unfortunately, American workers are traditionally wary of anything management proposes for their benefit.

Organizational Policy

The organizational policy dealing with alcoholism should be built upon the idea that treated alcoholics can be given back their full responsibilities. Punishment for the successfully recovered drinker should not be considered. Loyalty to the firm can be enhanced when it is known that the firm will stand by a worker and encourage his turn-around when his job and personal happiness are threatened.

The goal of the policy of rehabilitation is to avoid the economic loss that would be brought on if the firm had to hire another employee and sacrifice its investment in the alcoholic's training. One proponent of this attitude holds that the converted alcoholic often performs at better than his earlier predrinking level.

Like any new policy that management intends for more than lip service, the policy of the alcoholic rehabilitation program should be printed and made available to all employees. A good way to do this is through the departmental bulletin board or the personnel manual. A suggested policy reads in part:

Management has the same attitude toward the alcoholic as it does for anyone with another serious disease. We are not concerned whether an employee drinks at social gatherings, but when that worker's alcoholic consumption adversely effects his health or work, then management will become concerned.

4

Employee Problems with Gambling and Sex

GAMBLING AND SEX, like drug addiction and alcoholism, are personal problems of employees which can either originate in or carry over into the work environment. These types of behavior not only can make the individual personally less desirable as an employee but can adversely affect his productivity on the job.

Gambling on the Job

Some types of gambling are condoned by pactically all businesses; for example, management seldom frowns on a baseball pool conducted at World Series time. Gambling of this kind usually involves small sums of money and does not waste a great deal of employee time.

When gambling is allowed to go unchecked, however, it can become a serious problem for the business. The sums involved may get progressively larger, and the amount of time wasted can become a serious consideration. A worker who loses a considerable sum of money may concentrate all of his mental abilities on ways to recoup his losses. Moreover, an employee who loses a large share of his paycheck may be tempted to look around for company merchandise or property he can steal or pawn to recover his losses.

Most people who work have family responsibilities. Wives and children can suffer seriously if employees regularly lose any large proportion of their income.

If professional gamblers are allowed inside the business, the workers will be consistently cheated. In addition, "policy runners" and gambling bookies are frequently persons of poor character. If allowed to operate without supervision, they may be responsible for thefts or other crimes.

Card playing may be condoned by management in some types of jobs. For example, ramp service men (baggage handlers) at an airport may have considerable time on their hands between airline flights. In a situation of this kind management may agree to allow card games, provided no money changes hands and provided the game comes to a halt when there is work to be done. One of the problems with a situation of this kind is that it is often difficult to determine whether the game is a time-killing diversion or a game of chance. While no money may be passed from player to player, the participants may be maintaining mental records as to amounts owed other players from hand to hand.

Arbitration Decisions

The numbers racket, which makes use of policy runners, and race horse gambling, which often involves the placing of bets with bookies, are among the most common forms of gambling encountered in business and industrial installations. In a typical situation, an employee of an industrial firm made regular trips through production areas, collecting money for race bets from fellow workers. At noon he took the money and bets to a bookie at a neighborhood bar.

The company had a clearly worded rule, posted at many locations, prohibiting all employee gambling while on the job. After the employee's activities were noticed, he was discharged. The employee then filed for unemployment compensation, which was opposed by the company. Claiming that he was being discriminated against, the discharged employee pointed out that other individuals in the plant had gambled regularly but had not been disciplined.

When this matter came to arbitration, the discharged employee was refused his claim to unemployment pay. The labor arbitrator said that undoubtedly the discharged man had the right to take the money and bets to the bookie rather than spending his lunch hour in the company cafeteria, but he had been in the wrong in collecting the bets during working hours. Also, the arbitrator said, the discharged individual was guilty whether or not management saw fit to discipline those employees who had placed the bets.

In another case, two employees in the publication department of a New York City newspaper were arrested on warrants charging them with gambling violations. The next day, both of these men returned to work, stating that they had posted bail and were awaiting trial. Management declined to allow the two employees to resume work, stating that until their cases were disposed of, they were suspended without pay.

Both workers then maintained that they were innocent and that they intended to prove that they were not involved when the matter came to trial. The manager of the plant still did not let either of them come back to work, informing them that their suspensions would be lifted if they were acquitted but that they would be discharged if convicted.

More than eight weeks went by, and the cases against the two employees still had not been called for trail. The accused men pleaded for reinstatement, but the manager again refused to consider this request. A union representative then filed a grievance.

When the matter came before the arbitrator for a hearing, the union argued that the workers were being deprived of their right to make a living, even though they had not been found guilty of any criminal violation.

The upshot of this dispute was that the reinstatement of the two workers was ordered. The arbitrator pointed out that it was completely reasonable for the company to suspend them when the workers were first arrested, but the trial had been delayed for a considerable time, as is often the case in such court procedures. While the company was not at fault in any way, according to the arbitrator, it had no independent evidence of guilt concerning either of these persons. The arbitrator left the way open for the firm to discharge the two employees if they should be found guilty at the time of trial.

In a situation of this kind, there is nothing to prevent the company from launching an independent investigation of its own to determine the guilt or innocence of the men charged with the crime. The arbitrator's opinion indicates that he would not have ordered reinstatement had there been any reasonably substantiating evidence of guilt. If an investigation were conducted by management or the organization's security representative, management would have the right to discharge these employees if it was found that they were engaged in bookmaking while on company property. This would be an issue unrelated to the criminal prosecution, which would have little bearing on the company's decision here.

Controlling Employee Gambling

Gambling is extremely difficult to control merely by posting a rule. In general, arbitrators have upheld suspensions or dismissals for violations of company rules in this regard. However, a number of arbitrators have insisted that any antigambling policy must be applied to all the employees involved. The bettor, the bag man or money holder, and the runner all are to be disciplined when this approach is applied.

Union cooperation is usually essential in controlling gambling, and often it is easy to obtain. One reason is that union members are usually dependent on a paycheck for the welfare of their families. Another is that employees distracted by gambling do not contribute their share to productivity in meeting organizational goals. Some unions have been so cooperative in this area that they refuse to handle grievances for workers who are dismissed in clearly proven cases of gambling.

Work-Related Problems Involving Sex

Managers and supervisors may be inclined to discount the realities of sex in their company, despite the fact that sociologists generally agree that activities in any good-sized business or industrial installation will usually reflect the same cross section of activities, both normal and abnormal, that can be found in the surrounding community. Sex is no exception. In other words, the hiring process fails to create a sterile atmosphere in which sex no longer plays a part.

All firms, no matter how conservative, will lose productive time if female employees habitually dress in scanty or provocative costumes. This, of course, is one of the reasons some organizations insist that workers conform to a specified code of dress while on the job. In most instances, business is not concerned with the moralistic aspects of sex or any other personal matter. Profit-motivated companies realize that employees are most productive when they concentrate on work problems.

Sexual Incidents on the Job

It is not unknown for prostitutes to ply their trade inside a plant or warehouse. In one recent case, two portable vending vehicles were allowed entry to a business site to furnish food service to construction workers who were making an addition to a company structure. These vehicles were driven by two females who doubled as prostitutes for the construction workers. Some companies have found that camper vehicles on the company parking lot serve as convenient sites for sexual encounters, particularly for employees on late shifts.

Because an industrial uniform company had been experiencing repeated thefts of typewriters and other business machines, an official went to the plant at 4:00 A.M. to secretly observe the plant's opening procedures. Management wanted to learn whether the plant engineer was creating a continuing opportunity for theft by leaving the office area unlocked when he went to fire up the production room boilers. Shortly after the engineer came on the premises, it was observed that one of the female employees in the production department, who was not scheduled to report for work until 6:00 A.M., also entered the plant. A few minutes later the official found the engineer and the female employee in a compromising position.

Some firms ignore incidents of this kind because of fear that their reputations may be damaged. When such things are overlooked, however, there is the possibility that they may be discovered by outside authorities and magnified by news stories, with a great deal more embarrassment to the company. Management can never allow the use of business facilities for activities of this kind.

Sexual Involvement Away from the Job

An individual who becomes entangled in a sexual relationship with a co-worker away from the job poses another delicate situation for management. Involvement between an employee and an outside individual away from the job presents still another situation, but this is usually of concern to the firm only if it involves managerial workers in sensitive positions. Courts, arbitrators, and administrative agencies are inclined to view extramarital sex as of concern to no one but the individual employee.

In some instances this reasoning seems to be sound; an individual's private life is his own affair. Yet it is sometimes difficult to separate working hours from leisure pursuits. Almost imperceptibly, some outside affairs have a bearing on business operations. Nevertheless, if they do not directly affect the firm's productivity or profit structure, they are usually ignored by management. The loss of a valuable account could be considered the kind of activity that would justify employee discipline or dismissal.

Pornography

Pinup photographs of pretty girls are sometimes described as morale builders. They are harmless in themselves, but they are attention getters for male employees. Considerable unproductive time may result if employees are allowed to devote too much attention to them.

Approximately 200 companies in the country produce girlie magazines, pornographic comic books, and related photographs. Some firms allow employees in the production and warehouse areas to spend considerable time maintaining regular galleries and libraries of such material. In some cases, office reproduction facilities may be used to increase the circulation of ribald poems, books, or pictures. Some firms that are aware of this kind of activity tolerate it as a rather harmless employee diversion. But if people are allowed to study or read such material at work, there is little question that job efficiency will be reduced.

Obscene Graffiti

While no management representative need act as a guardian of morality or a censor, it is to management's advantage to maintain a wholesome atmosphere for the operation of its business. One problem in this regard is keeping walls and structures free of obscene drawings and slogans, particularly in rest rooms. A rest room used by the general public as well as workers particularly must be kept free of obscenities. Some firms have found it necessary to remove stall doors in employee rest rooms. Perhaps the most effective way to curtail this type of activity is to assign a janitorial or maintenance supervisor to make regular but unscheduled checks of rest room facilities.

When a new saying or drawing appears, it should be photographed and placed in a file maintained for comparison purposes. If it is observed shortly after completion, supervisors of nearby work areas may be able to limit responsibility to a small number of employees. As future incidents occur, it may be possible to determine culpability by eliminating names from the list if the people were known to have been at work when the drawing or writing was done. A number of cases of this sort have been solved by comparing photographs of handwriting or printing with writing samples available from employee personnel files. Distinctions in the way a suspect writes a specific letter of the alphabet or draws a certain item may indicate the artist.

Maintenance costs for removing a series of accumulated drawings may run from $400 to $500 for a single cleaning. Offenders have been known to use paint, tar, lacquer, lipstick, indelible pencil, or marking pens, or to scratch the message on stainless steel doors or accessories. One product that has been found helpful in removing marks from masonry walls is liquid sandblaster, a compound containing a solvent that will remove almost any kind of impression. The application of powerful chemicals of this kind usually requires repainting, however.

Obscene Communications or Notes

Female employees particularly may be recipients of obscene telephone calls or notes. The victims may be understandably reluctant to report such incidents. If the affair occurs while the worker is on the job or if it appears to be work related, management should take immediate interest in determining the perpetrators, and the police should be advised of all such instances.

Experience indicates that this kind of activity may continue indefinitely unless it is quickly and firmly stopped. If management expects to hire and retain respectable employees, obscene calls or notes cannot be tolerated.

5

Crimes on the Job:
Assault, Weapons, Threats

MANAGEMENT cannot afford to ignore any crimes committed on the job. For one thing, business success is dependent on a climate of order and stability. If it becomes known that crime is not reported, some workers will form the impression that management refuses to take a stand against other kinds of improper activity. Other employees may conclude, with justification, that this place of business is not a proper environment in which to work.

Management must also be aware that in a number of jurisdictions it is a criminal violation (misprision of felony) to fail to report a crime to police officials. This does not mean that management should engage in police investigations. Criminal aspects of the matter should be reported, cooperation should be offered, and the matter must then be left to the handling of the police and the courts.

In matters outside the scope of law enforcement, it is the duty of management to take immediate notice of any employee conduct that violates established company regulations or the rules of basic human decency. If employee misconduct involves both a criminal act and a violation of company regulations, then management has every right to discharge or to take other disciplinary action, regardless of the outcome of criminal charges.

Fighting on the Job

Any activity that interferes with the regular operating procedures of an industrial plant or business will result in loss. Fighting on the job is typical of the kind of disruptive activity that can seriously interfere with the realization of production goals. But the time lost by those involved in the fight is only part of the problem. Every employee who can see and hear the action will be disturbed, and the entire staff may be a long time in settling back into the routine.

There is general agreement that a worker may be fired for striking or assaulting a supervisor. Although an employee may claim that he struck the foreman, for example, without planning to do so, activity of this kind is generally regarded as inexcusable and is sufficient grounds for discharge.

It is human nature for employees to have differences with their fellows. Disagreements at the management and supervisory levels do not generally involve physical conflict. It is not unusual, however, for industrial or plant workers to actually come to blows.

No firm can function properly if the personnel are allowed to assault one another physically, regardless of the provocation. Safety, security, discipline, and employee morale all call for disputes to be settled without violence. The organization has the responsibility to preserve order and to protect workers from the risk of physical injury.

Such an attack is seldom committed without some reason. In the usual situation of this kind, one person picks on another, goading the latter until he loses his temper and strikes out. No one, of course, enjoys being subjected to taunts or insults. But galling as it may be, the proper procedure is for the victim to go to his supervisor and complain of the harassment, rather than swinging at his tormentor.

Forestalling Fighting

If supervisors become aware that there is a serious problem between two employees, it may be advisable to take immediate action to forestall an assault. In most instances fighting can be prevented by placing the two on different shifts or transferring one to a department where there is little likelihood that he or she will have any appreciable contact with the other party to the dispute.

It may also be helpful to interview both workers and advise them to break off contacts except when necessary in connection with their duties. Both employees could be counseled that disciplinary action will result immediately if further disruptions occur.

In any event, it is important for management to formulate a clearly worded rule pointing out that any individual who participates in a physical altercation is subject to immediate discharge. Like all rules, this policy must be publicized and made known to all employees.

Discharging Employees Involved in Fights

It is the usual policy in some firms to dismiss all individuals involved in a fight, without reference to which employee may have started the difficulty. The blanket application of this rule may be open to question. If the initial assault is made with a dangerous instrument, for example, the second employee may feel justified in defending himself to make certain that he is not seriously harmed. A blanket condemnation of all fighting may deny an employee the right of self-defense. For such reasons, and to avoid the pitfalls of generalization, it is suggested that management make sufficient inquiries to ascertain the facts of each incident before deciding to discharge the offenders.

In some situations one worker may be forced to fight to protect himself, while the other participant appears to be responsible for precipitating the incident. In instances of this kind, management may feel that the latter employee deserves to be discharged but the former is a satisfactory employee who should be retained in the company's best interests. If the employees are members of a labor union, it may be virtually impossible to fire one and retain the other. One approach in such instances is to discharge both employees but to rehire the worker who has satisfactory attitudes and a generally favorable work record.

Employees with Guns or Dangerous Weapons

Of even more concern to management are employees who carry firearms, knives, or other dangerous weapons to work. Because management is responsible for the safety of all employees, conditions that might jeopardize them cannot be allowed to go unchallenged.

The courts have consistently ruled that a firm has a right to prohibit the possession of weapons on its premises. Labor arbitrators also have usually held that an employee has no right to carry a weapon into his place of employment, particularly in violation of a clearly stated company rule. In specific cases, management was upheld in the right to fire a striker who packed a gun on a picket line, and management's discharge of a truck driver was affirmed when it was learned that he kept a gun in the cab of a company truck.

Another recent decision allowed the dismissal of an employee who was arrested on a charge of carrying an unlicensed gun on his person while driving on a public street. This ruling of the National Labor Relations Board was to the effect that firearms-carrying employees are undesirable, and management may discharge them for the safety of other workers.

Other cases do not go this far. In one instance, two female employees in an industrial plant engaged in a heated dispute, and the quarrel continued when they went to the company parking lot at the end of the shift. The facts are somewhat in dispute at that point, but one woman admitted she fired two shots from a pistol she carried on her person because the second female had pulled a knife on her. Both of the participants were arrested and convicted, one for shooting a gun within city limits in violation of a local ordinance and the second on a conviction of "menacing assault." The employee who had fired the gun was then discharged by her company.

An appeal was made to a labor arbitrator, who ruled that the woman should be reinstated, but without back pay. The arbitrator pointed out that there was no company rule in existence forbidding employees to bring firearms into the plant. In addition, it was noted that company personnel had previously sold guns in the factory during the lunch hour or break periods and that management was fully aware of this activity.

The Importance of Company Rules

The decision in the preceding case was apparently based on the fact that management was lax in prohibiting guns on company property. It is management's responsibility to post a clearly worded rule forbidding firearms from being carried into the plant or company facilities.

In a recent case the Caterpillar Tractor Company had posted a rule that appeared in the employee handbook as follows: "Firearms, explosives or liquor may not be carried into the plant at any time." An employee who owned a gun parked his motorcycle in the parking lot of the Caterpillar plant with a gun inside a rolled-up blanket strapped to the back of his bike. While in the parking lot, the employee was attacked by a nest of wasps. Grabbing the blanket (and the gun), he ran to the guard entrance to escape the stinging insects. The guard on duty took the gun and the blanket from the employee, who shortly after was discharged for violating the firm's rule against bringing firearms into the plant.

When the discharged employee asked for reinstatement and the matter came before a labor arbitrator, the company pointed out that the rule against firearms had been strictly enforced in the plant and was known to the employee in question. The labor union representing the employee maintained that the employee had not intended to bring the gun into the plant but only onto the company parking lot. In this instance the labor arbitrator ordered the reinstatement of the employee, on the basis that the company rule did not cover the parking lot.

It is difficult to justify the result reached in the Caterpillar case with those reached in some other cases. If there is any possibility for tension or physical violence in the surroundings of the establishment, it would be wise for management to publicize and enforce a rule to the effect that firearms may not be brought onto any part of company property, including company parking lots and recreation areas.

Exhibiting a Toy Gun

The threat of dangerous weapons to the order and stability of the work environment is so real that even the idea that one might be on the scene can be disruptive. In one case it was learned by management that an employee had pointed a gun at several other workers. While he did not fire the weapon, he caused considerable concern among those at whom he aimed. When confronted, the employee, claiming that the gun was merely a toy, went to his automobile and produced a toy pistol that closely resembled a real gun.

Because he had frightened fellow workers, this employee was discharged. A union grievance was filed demanding his reinstatement, but it was ruled that management was justified in discharging this individual.

Responsibility for Company Firearms

The courts have maintained that a firearm is an extremely dangerous device, and some police officials question whether guns should be owned by a company or maintained on its premises under any conditions. This is usually done only because the business is in a poor section of town and is apt to be robbed.

Security is essential for any gun maintained on the premises of a business or industry. Extreme care must be taken to prevent accidental death or injury through misuse of the weapons. If management is negligent in safeguarding the firearms, the firm may be answerable in damages to anyone who sustains harm through their misure. The fact that the manager or owner of the gun is legally licensed to possess it cannot be used as an excuse to avoid payment of damages if injury or death results from negligence.

Cases which have gone to arbitration have pointed out that it must be anticipated by management that workers may be curious about the operation of the gun and can accidentally injure themselves or others in handling it. Negligence cases consistently hold management responsible if the gun is left where it is easily available to juveniles or others who do not have the judgement necessary for handling firearms. Management is even more likely to be held negligent if the gun is left unguarded and fully loaded. In other situations, management has been held liable for failing to warn employees of the dangers attendant upon handling company weapons and for not issuing proper instructions regarding the use of the gun. Thus any firm that maintains firearms on its premises must take exceptional precautions to avoid harm.

Arming Security Guards

Many firms have a legitimate need to arm their security guards. While such guards must be allowed to utilize their weapons, the conditions under which they can do so must be clearly regulated. If the guard is physically attacked, for example, he may draw his weapon. State laws vary from jurisdiction to jurisdiction, but in most instances the guard would be justified in firing the weapon only in drastic circumstances.[1]

Although the company may feel that a security guard is justified in carrying a gun, there is seldom any reason for him to carry it when he is away from work. As a general rule all guard personnel should be required to check in their guns when they leave the job each day.

In one case an off-duty guard pulled a gun on another employee in a dispute outside the plant. The guard maintained that he had pulled the gun only in self-defense, but the facts indicated that the argument was a mere arm-waving situation at most. The company thereafter discharged the guard for poor judgment in using his gun. When the matter came to arbitration it was ruled that the company had the right to discharge the guard for this reason.[2]

---

[1] *Fawcett Printing Corporation* and *International Brotherhood of Teamsters, Chauffeurs, Warehousemen and Helpers of America, Local 89*, 71–2 ARB 8435.

[2] In re *Lockheed Aircraft Corporation* (Burbank, Calif.) and *International Association of Machinists*, Plant Protection Lodge 1638 (affiliated with Aeronautical Industrial Lodge 727, AFL, Grievance No. M–176, March 15, 1955, 20 LA 177.

Bomb Threat Telephone Calls

It is a criminal violation in many jurisdictions to make a telephone call threatening to bomb a home, school, business establishment, or any edifice. There is good reason to believe that employees are responsible for the majority of bomb threat telephone calls made to business and industry. A shift worker at a manufacturing plant, for example, may make a call of this nature in the belief that he or she will be paid in full for working only part of a shift. Such calls may originate with employees who have a grudge against management, or they may be placed by emotionally disturbed employees or ex-employees.

The intent to make such a telephone call is the criminal violation in most instances of this kind. It is immaterial whether the person making the call actually intended to go through with the threat.

In one case that came to trial, an employee of a hospital made a call to an acquaintance on the front desk reporting that a bomb had been secreted someplace within the building and would go off in 15 minutes. While this incident was intended to be a practical joke, it was taken seriously by the employee who received the call. Observing the consternation that resulted, the woman who had originated the call immediately notified a security guard that her intention had been completely misinterpreted. The caller was then arrested and charged with making a false bomb threat.

When the matter came to trial, the employee's claim that she had merely intended to play a prank on an acquaintance was disallowed. A conviction resulted and was upheld in the appellate court. In commenting on this decision, the Ohio Court of Appeals pointed out that it was not necessary for the caller to have the intent to place a bomb. The only intent required for conviction was that of making the call in question, irrespective of the motive behind the telephoned message.[3]

---

[3] *Langley* v. *State*, 288 NE 2d 334.

Several cases illustrate the value of including a clause in the union contract providing that workers shall be paid only for the hours actually worked in the event of a shutdown because of a bomb threat. In one, a production plant was shut down after a call was received stating that there were six sticks of dynamite in the assembly department. Like many others of this kind, the call proved to be a hoax. In order to protect employees, however, the work shift was canceled and the employees were sent home.

Under this firm's contract with the union, employees were entitled to reporting pay for four hours' work in the event that work was available. When this matter came to arbitration, it was ruled that management would be required to pay each employee for reporting, regardless of the fact that the shift had been canceled for the employees' safety.

In a somewhat similar incident, a manufacturing plant was shut down for the protection of employees after a bomb threat call was received. In this case, however, the company had a contract with the union which specified that the firm was not required to furnish reporting pay in the event of a fire, flood, disaster, major mechanical breakdown, or conditions beyond the control of the company. This occurrence also came to arbitration, and the arbitrator ruled that the bomb threat was clearly an emergency beyond the control of the company. Under these circumstances, the firm was not required to provide reporting pay for time after the workers were sent home.[4]

Another industrial plant was plagued by a series of bomb threat calls. After two of these threats turned out to be false, management refused to close down the plant. Employees were advised that they could work if they desired, or they could go home.

This case came up for arbitration when employees claimed that they should be paid for the balance of the shift even though they

---

[4] In re *Goodyear Tire and Rubber Co.* (Dallas, Texas) and *Dallas General Drivers, Warehousemen and Helpers (IBT), Local 745,* FMCS Case No. 71A/1626, December 23, 1970, 55 LA 1119.

went home. The labor arbitrator ruled for the company, pointing out that the company was somewhat at the mercy of employees in a situation of this kind. The arbitrator noted that if he ruled otherwise, the company could be forced to pay out money regularly at the whim of any mischief maker who continued to make telephoned threats.

The most serious crime problem in business and industry is not concerned with assault, weapons, or threats, however. It is employee theft, the subject of the following chapter.

6

Employee Theft

EMPLOYEES at all levels may be involved in theft. Often there are no readily apparent differences between individuals who steal or pilfer and thousands of other employees. Actual cases indicate that many of these inside crimes are committed by trusted employees, those who have the greatest opportunity to do so and are the last to be suspected.

Some so-called experts are regularly quoted as to the millions of dollars that are lost annually by business because of employee thefts. While such loss figures are estimates at best and cannot be substantiated, the reported losses to business and industry on account of employee theft are staggering. Moreover, many such crimes go undetected or unreported.

Employees who steal can be classified as basically either "object" thieves or "money" thieves. There are no figures to measure accurately how losses in the two categories compare. Some insurance authorities have set the value of merchandise losses as approximately seven times that of the cash taken in recent years.

The direct financial losses that can be attributed to employee theft are only the most obvious costs. There are other consequences that are equally harmful for business. When thefts occur, insurance costs go up. Sales may be lost, and customer goodwill is often damaged. When stock items are stolen and orders cannot be filled, customers look to other sources of supply.

Company morale may also suffer. Self-respecting employees may not want to work alongside others they know to be thieves. And management may lose the respect of rank-and-file employees if it becomes obvious that it either does not care or lacks the ability to control such a situation.

Management's Responsibility for Theft Control

Any company that hires a large number of employees can expect to be faced with the problems of employee theft. There are no reliable methods for recruiting only honest employees or preventing them from performing dishonest acts once they are hired. But if a company is consistently troubled by employees who steal, then management must bear a good part of the responsibility. Dishonesty is frequently the product of bad management.

Underlying management's control of crime is the fact that opportunities for theft are often created and condoned by management itself. These opportunities seldom arise by chance. When it is obvious that internal controls are lacking or that attention is not being given to putting into practice the controls that have been formulated on paper, theft problems can be predicted with reasonable accuracy.

The Influence of Management Attitudes

Company officials should never underestimate their ability to promote honest performance in employees. There are many ways management can make workers aware of the value the firm places on integrity. The basic objective is to ensure fair and reasonable accountability by company representatives in all aspects of the business.

To set the example, managers and supervisors themselves should faithfully observe all written agreements or verbal promises that have been given to workers. By the integrity of their own performance they can demonstrate that dishonesty is intolerable. For example, managers should never ignore the company rule that items taken from the stockroom must be signed for, nor should they allow themselves three-hour lunches while insisting that production employees be disciplined or penalized for exceeding their assigned lunch period.

Management's attitudes toward customer orders can also be influential in that moment of decision when an employee finds himself faced with the temptation to steal. The example can be set by management's insistence that shoddy merchandise never be shipped or that shipping counts never be short, for instance. Supervisors and managers unconsciously exhibit their real feelings about honesty by the attitudes they display toward company controls. The manager who does not take short cuts in auditing control procedures, who consistently uses security devices, and who follows established procedures in merchandise handling is telling rank-and-file workers that the firm is concerned with honesty in all its operations. To some workers, management indifference is a license to steal.

The existence of crime in the business world does not justify the rationalization that employee theft must be accepted as a cost of doing business. It is a mistake for management to make compromises where theft is concerned. It cannot neglect to discharge any employee discovered in theft for reasons such as the facts that the individual involved is a hard worker or the item stolen is of little value. It is questionable judgment to set a level of theft above which one employee will be discharged and below which another will be allowed to remain on the payroll.

A rationalization can also be made that dishonesty is so widespread in society in general that it can never be eliminated. But a private company does not have to contend with many of the uncontrollable factors that influence society at large. In the first place, the private employer has a choice as to which applicant he hires. He can also exercise control over the physical environment in which the business is located, and he can install procedural controls under which all workers must function. Loss from theft can therefore be controlled considerably by management choice.

Why Employees Steal

It cannot be said with certainty what causes any individual to participate in a theft. However, there are three conditions that seem to exist in a great many cases. These are:

1. The thief has an ego need which he feels must be satisfied, irrespective of his real physical needs.
2. The thief is able to justify his activity in his own mind.
3. The thief has access to the money or property taken, frequently because of a breakdown in management controls.

The Thief's Perceived Need

Very few individuals in the United States must steal to prevent hunger. Nevertheless, the thief feels a "need" he must satisfy. Some individuals do have more financial need than others, but in most cases the need to steal is an ego need. The rationalization to steal is real in the mind of the thief. He may steal to fulfill his need for adventure or status in his group, or he may have a personal problem which motivates him to seek financial help but which does not seem to be pressing by the standards of others. Such a thief has a mental picture of what he feels he must have, whether or not he has the money to afford it. For example, he may be convinced that he cannot maintain stature with his close associates unless he has a costly set of golf clubs.

In most cases, if the employee who steals were honest with himself, he would admit that he does not really require the article he has his mind set on. Nevertheless, he often regards the need as completely essential. The basis for the need may be to maintain a marital relationship in which either husband or wife refuses to acknowledge the financial limitations on their income, or it could be motivated by a problem the thief regards as unsharable. His solution to such problems is theft, although he cannot justify any such need.

Justification by the Thief

Few people will admit even to themselves that they are dishonest. The thief explains away such actions on the basis that he is entitled to more from the company or from society as a whole than he has been given or has earned for himself.

By the same type of reasoning, the thief may assert that he is only taking something to compensate for unpaid overtime or a delayed pay raise. The employee who steals frequently rationalizes that "everybody else does it" or that the firm he works for has plenty of assets and will never miss the little he needs.

Lack of Controls by Management

Opportunity for theft is frequently provided by the firm's failure to implement management controls. It can be expected that if management does not go to the trouble of exercising control, money or property will be taken. When controls are ignored by company officials, employees form the impression that the owners and managers simply do not care. In most instances, losses do not occur because of lack of controls but because these controls are not regularly audited and results assessed.

Knowing the Living Habits of Employees

Every employee of any organization has the right to live his own life as he chooses. Management officials have long recognized, however, that knowledge of the personal habits and activities of workers may be a tipoff concerning those who could be engaged in embezzlement or theft. In 1863, Hugh McCulloch, the first U.S. Comptroller of the Currency, instructed the managers of all U.S. national banks as follows:

Pay your officers such salaries as will enable them to live comfortably and respectably without stealing; and require of them their entire services. If any officer lives beyond his income, dismiss him; even if his excess of expenditures can be explained consistently with integrity, still dismiss him. A man cannot be a safe officer of a bank who spends more than he earns.

Some managers may feel that the stringent ideas expressed by McCulloch are still valid. The problem is that many companies now hire thousands of workers, and it is almost impossible to have complete knowledge of the personal habits of all of them.

Supervisors, however, often have intimate knowledge of the living standards and requirements of their own workers, even in large organizations. Supervisors will naturally be reluctant to participate in spying on personal habits, and there are cases in which a worker may have other sources of income unknown to his supervisor. But if it clearly appears that an employee is living beyond his income, management can be advised confidentially without doing an injustice to the individual worker.

Attitudes toward Theft

To an employer, theft by workers, even of small amounts or an inexpensive item, is an offense of such magnitude that immediate discharge is usually justified. To the employee, however, this appears to be an overly severe penalty, because workers released for dishonesty may find it difficult or almost impossible to get a new job.

Some employees will concede that discharge is warranted in cases where employees steal for personal gain. However, a considerable amount of this kind of stealing is a psychological reaction to companies which control the activities of employees by coercive authority. In such an organization, a supervisor issues orders and rewards or punishes employees according to the way in which they follow his instructions. Controls of this kind may achieve short-run results, but they also can cause problems because the worker sees the supervisor as opposing rank-and-file employees in an adversary system.

It becomes a challenge, on at least an occasional basis, for employees to prove to themselves that they can get the best of the supervisor. A game sometimes results in which workers steal to prove that they can get away with it, as a challenge to the supervisor, or to break the monotony of their routine. At times there may be an element of revenge, or the employee may rationalize that his dishonest act was not actual dishonesty.

An employee detected in one of these psychologically motivated situations almost invariably feels that discharge is far too harsh a penalty. The worker in a union plant customarily seeks shelter in the grievance procedures set up in the union contract. In most instances he does not expect to be excused but rather to avoid outright discharge and to be able to regain some measure of respectability.

There is reluctance on the part of some labor arbitrators to uphold a dismissal for theft reasons, especially if the offender may be a marked man in his efforts to obtain employment. In recent years, arbitrators have sometimes softened the penalty, ordering reinstatement with loss of pay, restitution to the company for the property stolen, and loss of some employee privileges.

Management seldom discharges in a situation of this kind out of hardness of heart. Rather, the step is taken to rid the company of an employee who is almost certain to cause further loss unless his activities can be curtailed. Labor arbitrators who are socially oriented often look for a way to sever the thief from the company payroll without branding him as unemployable. When a route drive stole collections that had been received by drivers on other routes, one arbitrator ruled that the offender could be discharged for "consistent inability to handle collections." Others have been fired for "failure to follow proper procedures," or for "gross carelessness in handling company merchandise."

Sustaining Discharge in Arbitration Hearings

It is almost always in management's interests to let employees know that they can expect immediate discharge if they are found guilty of theft. If a case goes to arbitration, there is a good possibility that discharge may not be upheld if management has been lax in this regard or has exhibited a compromising attitude toward theft in the past.

In one instance, bus drivers had cheated the company they worked for until it had become something of a way of life for them. When the company discovered and discharged one of these offending drivers, a labor arbitrator reinstated the driver and directed strong criticism against the company for its action.

A routeman involved in a somewhat similar activity presented testimony at his arbitration hearing to the effect that management had been aware that routemen were pocketing company money for over a year and had done nothing about it. In this instance, the routeman was suspended for several months but was allowed to return to work.

Decisions of this nature indicate that management cannot ignore cases of theft until losses reach burdensome levels, and then crack down at will. If a company has been easygoing in the past, it must first warn workers, clearly and emphatically, that a change in policy is to be instituted. Thereafter, management should regularly post notices on company bulletin boards advising that the penalty for theft is immediate dismissal. Alternatives would be to print notices in the company house organ and rule book or announce them at scheduled departmental and sectional meetings for employees. It is also appropriate for the company to advise union representatives that the penalty will be enforced for future infractions.

Can an Employee Be Discharged for Theft Even If Acquitted?

In a recent California case, an employee was suspected of stealing merchandise from a supermarket. To resolve this suspicion, the company hired two private investigators to observe activities near the rear of the store. They saw four store employees, including the suspect, come out of the rear door and place grocery bags in their own automobiles. Three of them returned to the store, while the suspect drove away from the scene.

When the three individuals returned to the store, they were confronted with the fact that the sacks they had carried out contained groceries, and they admitted that they had stolen the merchandise from the store. It was not possible for the investigators to examine the contents of the bag carried out by the original suspect, but he did admit carrying a package from the store.

All four of the employees were charged with petty theft, and the three who had made admissions were found guilty and placed on probation. The original suspect maintained that he was innocent and flatly contradicted the testimony of the investigators who had observed the activity. The court acquitted the suspect.

Not satisfied with his victory in court, the suspect returned to the supermarket and demanded to be reinstated on his old job. He subsequently filed a grievance and took the matter to arbitration. The arbitrator ruled that the suspect had no right to reinstatement, pointing out that the evidence clearly showed he had removed the groceries and that acquittal had only excused him from the criminal aspects of his act.

Is an Attempted Theft Sufficient Cause for Discharge?

A provision frequently inserted in labor contracts stipulates that "Employee theft or pilfering shall be just cause for immediate dismissal." Even if the theft is not actually completed, in some cases arbitrators have held that an attempted theft is just as serious as one that is fully carried out, and an attempt justifies dismissal. The fact that his activities are interrupted by management vigilance does not in any way excuse the dishonest employee.

In a recent case, however, two workers were ordered reinstated when the evidence against them was obtained in a search by security men who worked for an adjoining business. Attorneys for the two workers under suspicion claimed that the search that uncovered the evidence was illegal and that it therefore could not be used for discharge. This result seems to be completely out of line with other decisions. In most instances, private companies have been justified in discharging dishonest employees, even if legal technicalities resulted in their acquittal in criminal court.

Can an Employee Be Discharged or Suspended for Refusing to Furnish Information?

Under the Fifth Amendment to the Constitution, no one can be compelled to testify against himself or to incriminate himself. This right is recognized and protected by both state and local courts.

But this right is to protect against criminal prosecution, not to guarantee a right to employment. In a recent case on this point an employee declined to furnish company officials with information about a warehouse shortage. Facts that were developed independently indicated that the employee was in possession of pertinent information and was possibly involved himself. The employee based his refusal to talk on the claimed right to be protected under the Fifth Amendment.

A labor arbitrator ruled that the company had the right to discharge the employee for his failure to cooperate in providing information. The arbitrator added that employers have a right to absolute honesty as well as cooperation from their employees.

In a somewhat similar case, an employee in a production plant agreed to furnish information about how merchandise was being stolen from the warehouse in exchange for a payment of $50. When the money was furnished by management, the informer stated that he had seen two employees secrete merchandise inside floor drains. The merchandise was subsequently removed from the hiding place by employees outside the warehouse. However, the informant declined to reveal the names of the employees he had observed.

The company then suspended the informant for failure to cooperate with management. Arbitration followed a union request for reinstatement. The arbitrator ruled that the employee had no right to reinstatement unless he disclosed the names of the persons he had seen secrete the merchandise. The arbitrator also decided that the company must agree to protect the informant from both lawsuits and employee reprisals should it take any action on the information.[1] In this connection, arbitrators have quite uniformly held that an employee has an obligation not to withold information from management concerning dishonesty or theft by co-workers.[2]

---

[1] *Simoniz Company* and *International Chemical Workers Union, Local 559*, 65–1 ARB 8355.

[2] In re *Eisen Merchantile, Inc.* and *International Brotherhood of Teamsters, Chauffeurs, Warehousemen and Helpers of America, Local 956*, February 10, 1972, 58 LA 340.

The Decision to Prosecute

Some firms prosecute all employees who are caught in company thefts or embezzlements. Others immediately discharge the guilty employee, reasoning that the discharge and disgrace will be punishment enough. Some companies fear that the firm's image may be tarnished if officials or employees are prosecuted, and others do not want to risk the possibility of a lawsuit if the prosecution should be unsuccessful.

If a bonded employee is detected in a theft or embezzlement, prosecution may be initiated by the bonding company, in spite of the employer's desires about prosecution. Many security officials with a law enforcement background seem to believe that company thieves should be prosecuted as an example to others. There is a general difference of opinion, however, as to the effectiveness of prosecution as a deterrent. It is costly in terms of management hours spent in court, and the question is open to argument.

In an Arizona case, a woman clerk confessed to thefts from a store, but only after the store manager promised her that she would be spared prosecution and embarrassment if she would admit guilt. The president of the company thereafter insisted that the clerk be criminally prosecuted. When the matter came to trial, the court ruled that the confession could not be used as evidence.[3] This seems to be a settled rule of law, that a confession induced by a promise of immunity from the employer is inadmissible.

---

[3] *State of Arizona* v. *Hess,* 449 P 2d 46.

7

Employee Purchases and Gifts to Employees

MOST RETAIL ESTABLISHMENTS allow their own employees to buy any merchandise that is kept in stock, usually at a discount. Some manufacturers and wholesalers also permit employee purchases, although they normally do not sell to the retail trade. Many workers feel strongly that this is a benefit due them. Sales of this kind are thought to have a favorable effect on employee morale, especially when an employee discount is allowed.

One of the largest airlines in the United States not only allows its personnel to utilize the company's services for low-cost travel, but it also permits workers to buy any of the items kept in the firm's warehouses or stockrooms at a reduced cost. An official of the airline explained that this unusual position had been adopted because "Employees may be tempted to steal whatever they feel they need, if they are not allowed to buy it. Our employee purchase system leaves employees with a sense of honesty that seems to carry over into other aspects of their jobs."

Some companies are opposed to allowing sales to their own

workers, however. Generally, two reasons are advanced for taking this position:

1. The profit margin from this kind of transaction is minimal at best, especially where discounts are granted to employees, and the special handling of merchandise and payments will not justify the additional effort that is required.
2. Loss experiences have resulted too frequently to make it feasible to grant this benefit to employees.

One company that found an employee purchase plan to be unsuccessful had allowed all employees to take home without charge a personal supply of the razor blades it produced. It came to the attention of management that the rank and file were helping themselves to blades greatly in excess of their personal requirements. When the company investigated it was found that workers were selling large quantities of blades through neighborhood bars, and the benefit was then discontinued.

If substantial discounts are allowed to employees who make purchases, it can be anticipated that company personnel will sometimes buy products for their friends and relatives. This is often regarded as objectionable from a company standpoint, as it generally represents lost profits. Too frequent buying for outside friends may lead to a discontinuance of the employee privilege.

Selling Damaged Merchandise to Employees

Some firms provide employees with an opportunity to purchase products with small flaws or defects that make them unacceptable to customers. This not only pleases the worker, but it makes it possible to obtain some revenue from products that would otherwise be written off as a loss. In some cases sales of damaged or shopworn items are held on a regular basis. In others a manager or supervisor is given authority to mark down an obviously flawed article on the spot.

Unless carefully supervised, however, this practice can be abused, and this kind of employee sale can work against the company. Employees may be tempted to deliberately scratch or damage whatever they want to buy at a markdown. Sometimes the replacement of only a small part or a minor component could make an item acceptable for customer sale. In companies that frequently sell damaged stock to their personnel it has been found that some workers are reluctant to make repairs or to replace damaged components and thereby make an article salable. This could, of course, contribute to the loss picture.

Experiences of this nature have led some firms to follow a policy of selling new merchandise to employees but refusing to sell damaged items. Firms that do not allow employee purchases may dispose of unsalable merchandise by giving the entire lot to charity or junking it in a trash bin. To make certain that such merchandise is not taken from the trash, they may smash the articles before throwing them away. Other companies dispose of this type of merchandise by sale to a contract salvage company after the stock has accumulated for a considerable time.

Processing Employee Purchases

Employees are sometimes allowed to select and package their own purchases on the honor system. Numerous instances can be documented in which employees have paid for a single item and then added merchandise to the package as the day went on. It is sometimes argued that such workers are not hardened thieves but have succumbed to the temptations of a weakly controlled system.

The company administrative manual for a New York firm stipulates that "Any employee purchase shall be handled as any other order." Customers are not allowed to select and wrap their own merchandise, and neither should employees be. But merely prohibiting employees from selecting and wrapping their own purchases may not be enough. The manager of a San Francisco store recently observed two retail clerks selling items to each other at about one tenth of the listed price. A requirement that all employee sales be verified and approved by supervisors might have eliminated this kind of loss.

Firms which do not allow employees to package their own purchases nevertheless may condone their taking packages to work areas after securing the sacks with a stapling machine. Sometimes the sales slip is also stapled to the sack containing the purchase. This control is often of doubtful value, as it is relatively easy to add more merchandise in most instances. Instead of adding items to those already purchased, some employees substitute a similar article of greater value for one they have paid for.

To prevent additions or substitutions to employee packages, some firms require advance submission of a purchase list to department heads, who arrange for selections. A workable system of this kind may call for setting a deadline for employee purchases, after which a stock clerk makes all requested selections. After orders have been filled and packaged, they can be kept at a specified pickup point.

A recommended follow-up of this system calls for all packages to be retained at a central control desk until payment has been verified on the sales slip and delivery has been made to the employee. The original of the sales ticket should be marked "paid," if this is the case, and a duplicate kept at the pickup desk for accounting or security verification.

It is important that the employee not be allowed to take his package back to a work area for the remainder of the day. Ideally, he should pick up purchased merchandise at the time he concludes the work shift. This can best be accomplished by having the pickup made at a location just inside the building, at the employee's exit. A rule should be in effect prohibiting the employee from coming back into the building with his purchase.

Charging Employee Purchases

If the employee does not pay cash for his purchases, the cost may be deducted from his pay check. This system is generally satisfactory, but care must be exercised to make certain that the sales slip cannot be pulled out and destroyed. If this happens, business loss results from failure to bill the employee. It is thereafter essential that employees who make purchases of this nature should not be given access to their own charge slips.

A suggested control involves the use of prenumbered employee credit sales tickets, with each ticket or charge slip accounted for numerically. These tickets should be treated as cash and afforded the same protection.

In one case reported not long ago in New York State, a highly placed executive sold company merchandise to employees under the firm's employee purchasing plan, which allowed the sale of merchandise at a considerable discount. The problem was that the executive never reported the sales and personally collected the amounts due from employees. He maintained a private set of books with notations as to employee purchases made, how much had been paid, and the balance still owing. This set of books, of course, eventually assisted in providing proof of his misconduct.

Gifts to Company Employees

Every firm has a right to object to gifts given to its employees. This is only good business. The worker who receives a gratuity from an outside firm may unconsciously favor that company, sometimes to the detriment of his own. This is particularly true of buyers, who may give outright favoritism to suppliers that charge prices that are not in line with those of their competition.

An employee who exercises discretion in purchasing for his company must not be influenced by such outside factors. His own company's interests must come first. If the purchasing agent is allowed to accept gifts, it may be very hard for management to determine whether his judgment has been unduly influenced.

Some businesses follow a rule that requires every employee to advise management of the receipt of any gift. This rule is usually qualified to permit the employee to receive a gift of nominal value, sales samples, or advertising matter. The acceptance of small tokens of goodwill has long been a commonplace business practice.

Because of the problem of undue influence, many companies send a form letter to suppliers at least once a year stating that gifts cannot be received by their representatives. Such letters are often mailed immediately prior to the Christmas–New Year season. Some companies that follow this practice refuse to accept any presents of this kind on which delivery is attempted.

Receiving a Gift without Being Influenced

Time and again the purchasing agent for a company in a southwestern state accepted gratuities from one of his firm's vendors. These gifts did not represent the expenditure of a great deal of money, and the agent himself did not feel that his judgment had been swayed in receiving them.

When the acceptance of these gifts was accidentally revealed, the agent's employer discharged him and tore up his employment contract. The agent sued for the value of his contract and lost. When the case was appealed, the court ruled for the employer, agreeing that the undisclosed acceptance of gifts alone would be sufficient grounds for discharge of the agent. The court noted that any activity on the part of the agent that was "calculated to destroy the confidence of a reasonable employer would justify his discharge as purchasing agent—whether the misconduct caused the business to suffer actual loss or not."[1]

When Does a Gift Become a Bribe?

When would reasonable businessmen agree that a bribe has been offered to a purchasing agent? Most companies will not be troubled if a supplier treats a buyer to a drink or two and pays the dinner check for the buyer and his wife. But practically all companies object to the passing of money or presents of more than nominal worth. If the purchasing agent's judgment could have been affected, the actual value of the gift or the amount of money passed to him is of no consequence. The damage has been done, because this is outright bribery.

Eighteen or more states have passed laws defining this type of activity as a criminal offense. Under the wording of these statutes, the soliciting, offering, receiving, or giving of anything of value to influence action is a violation.

But even if this kind of activity is not a crime under state law, it is a civil wrong against the firm represented by the purchasing agent. A lawsuit can be pursued, both against the company offering the bribe and the purchasing agent accepting it. In those cases where bribery is subsequently uncovered, the courts of some states do not permit the supplier to receive payment or to sue for the value of the merchandise that was furnished. The courts in other states do permit the supplier to recover the sales price of the goods but require the supplier to clearly prove that actual value was given to the buyer.[2]

---

[1] *Wade* v. *William Barr Dry Goods Co.,* 134 SW 1084.

[2] *Sirkin* v. *Fourteenth Street Store,* 108 NY Supp. 830.

Determining Whether Prices Paid Are Competitive

To eliminate the possibility of kickbacks to a purchasing agent, some companies obtain competitive bids for many kinds of supplies and merchandise and make certain that from time to time a nonstandard vendor is allowed to bid on delivery prices for these items.

In general, it is good procedure for management to take an active interest in verifying purchase invoices, both as to the quality of goods delivered and the prices paid for them.

An additional technique used by some firms is to advise the head of each department of the price paid for the items he has requested. In many companies department heads are frequently aware of the going prices for many of the things they use and will advise management if prices paid are excessive.

8

Misuse of Company
Facilities or Property

IT MAY SEEM trifling for management to be concerned with employee misuse of copying machines, mail room facilities, or other available conveniences. Individually, the costs resulting from the abuse of such facilities may be small, but the cumulative effect of such losses can be considerable.

Copying Machines

In many firms it is common practice for employees to use the copying machine for their own purposes. The possibility should not be discounted that this activity may involve the secret duplication of sensitive company information for the use of a business competitor. Most unauthorized use of the copying machine, however, concerns nothing more sinister than reproducing a Boy Scout list, PTA information, or an out-of-print novel. Occasionally this may be sanctioned on the basis that it is good public relations. Uncontrolled use, however, can become very costly.

Perhaps the majority of businesses do allow some usage for

personal reasons. If an employee needs one copy of his birth certificate or wants to retain a duplicate of some document he regards
as important, copying is generally permitted. Reasonable usage
of this kind can improve employee morale. But a line must be
drawn at some point where personal usage of copying equipment
is considered excessive, as in making several hundred copies of
a program for a social organization.

The secretary of a San Francisco banker caused embarrassment
to her institution when she revealed that she had been duplicating
an issue of *Playboy* magazine for her supervisor. At a major scientific firm in Michigan, middle-management employees are frank
to state that they use their firm's copying equipment in duplicating
long scientific papers for their own personal files. Another misuse
of the office copying machine is the running off of personal re-
sumés by job-hunting employees or executives. This type of activity is particularly annoying to management because such employees are using company facilities to seek jobs with competing
firms.

Most copying machines are lockable and can be secured at
night. If it is not necessary to use the machine on the night shift,
it is suggested that the machine be locked and that a reading
be taken of the number of copies made at the close of the daytime
shift. Comparison with the starting figure the following morning
can ascertain whether misuse is occurring at night.

Small organizations have found that the copy machine is seldom
misused if it is located within the view of a supervisor, and a
regulation requiring supervisory approval for more than ten copies
or ten pages has been found effective by some companies. A major
U.S. airline office reduced the average number of copies made
per month by approximately 200,000 by requiring all copies made
to be entered on a log and all usage to be approved by supervision.
Management, however, must strike a balance between the savings

achieved and the amount of time that may be lost in obtaining supervisory authorization for making copies.

Credit Cards

An employee has an obligation to safeguard the company's credit cards, just as he must make certain that all cash and other assets are properly accounted for. It is advisable to educate employees to the possibility of theft and misuse of company credit cards, so that lost cards will be reported promptly.

A basic requirement for preventing loss is to issue credit cards only on the basis of need. A regular program to review outstanding credit cards can be helpful in preventing loss. If an employee has no need to travel to Europe, for example, it is pointless to furnish him with a type of card that will authorize travel to another part of the world.

In one actual situation, a relatively new sales employee used his company telephone credit card to charge over 100 personal long distance calls in a period of about six months. The employee did not realize that spot checks would be made to verify the accuracy of telephone company charges. When confronted with the facts, the employee first claimed that someone had misused his card or that the telephone company had made a series of errors. The employee was discharged when it was ascertained that he had been at the towns from which each of the calls was made at approximately the time stated in the telephone company records.

After his discharge, the salesman appealed to arbitration. The arbitrator ruled that the company was completely justified in his discharge, reasoning that failure to protect company assets, as represented by the credit card, is a type of embezzlement for which there is no excuse.

Company Telephones

A common source of loss for many companies is the employee who makes unauthorized long distance calls. The best way to identify calls of an unauthorized nature is by checking each item on the long distance telephone bill. This can involve an expenditure of considerable administrative time unless the firm is extremely small or does not utilize the telephone to any great extent.

Some firms make it difficult for employees to use telephone equipment at night by disconnecting all but a few key executive telephones that operate through a central switchboard. Others have endeavored to fix responsibility with the departments and individuals making telephone calls by use of a Centrex system which identifies the unit over which the long distance call was made. This system is not always effective, since an employee may utilize the extension of a department other than his own or one that has no employees on duty.

Some firms have solved this problem by placing an inexpensive lock on the dialing arrangement at the close of business. This is a time-consuming operation, however, if any appreciable number of telephone extensions are available. Still other companies make arrangements whereby any long distance conversation must go through a central operator who maintains a brief form recording the name of the employee making the call and the reason for the communication.

Some management employees argue that it is inefficient and stifling to place too many restrictions on officials who have a real need to make calls and who have sufficient authority to do so without question. The cost of excessive controls through extensive record keeping may be greater than the savings achieved by preventing unauthorized calls. In any event, one of the most effective controls may be to require that employees who have no assigned duties in the building at night register on an entry log, reflecting the time of entry and departure and the reason for being in the building.

Mail Room Facilities

Some employees send all their Christmas cards and packages, or even all their personal mail, using company mail facilities. If management will go to the trouble to make spot checks of the outgoing mail, this misuse can be revealed easily. A company rule should be in effect calling for employee discipline if mail facilities are used for personal convenience.

Some firms have also found that if mail room employees are allowed to sell postage stamps to others, they may overlook collecting for the cash or pocket it. If stamps are retained under lock and key and regular audits are made, control of this item can be maintained. Many firms utilize a postage meter not only for convenience but because employees are less inclined to misuse the meter than to carry away stamps that can be used at home. Locking the postage meter at night is a recommended technique for avoiding loss. Unless this is done, anyone who has access could run off a hundred or more postage strips without attracting attention.

Some companies have found that substantial sums can be saved by making sure that mail room employees do not use larger denominations of stamps than are necessary and that scales are used to weigh all packages and those letters that may require extra postage. A quick check of outgoing mail by management in one company disclosed that many packages and letters were carrying more postage than necessary. It was learned that frequently the mail clerk did not take the time to weigh doubtful letters or packages but merely added an extra stamp because "it never hurts to be on the safe side."

Training periods can also reduce mail room costs by teaching employees to use the correct class of mail service needed in sending a particular piece of mail. For example, if advertising matter is not clearly marked as third class and left unsealed, it will be handled as first class mail by the post office. The material may be returned for additional postage, or the individual receiving the communication may be charged for postage due, creating an unfavorable impression. Air mail may also be used excessively unless there is occasional examination of the outgoing mail by someone in supervision.

Some firms retain a cash fund in the mail room for the payment of C.O.D. charges or postage due and for other contingencies. If a safe is available, these funds should be retained in the safe at night and in a locked cashbox during working hours. Auditing controls should be similar to those used for petty cash funds (see Chapter 9), and receipts should be reviewed to make certain that the amounts have not been raised or altered.

Parcel delivery services are increasingly being used to make shipments of small items from company stockrooms or warehouses. Employees may be tempted to take advantage of this system to ship merchandise to a friend or to their own address without paying for the goods. Management can make a comparison of the number of boxes picked up with the number of shipping tickets on hand. If it is found that the two are not in balance, an excess number of packages over tickets may represent merchandise items being embezzled, stolen, or consigned to a friend with whom an employee is in collusion.

A regular program for monitoring parcel shipments of this kind can be a valuable management tool in avoiding loss. It is suggested that verifications of this kind be made without prior notice and at irregular times, so that a dishonest employee will have no advance warning that the audit is to be made.

It may also be worth noting that many firms receive large numbers of incoming checks in the mails. There is always a possibility that incoming company checks could be removed by an employee for diversion to his own use. This will usually be discovered when the customer protests the receipt of a second statement, pointing out that he has already sent in a check in payment, but a dishonest employee may be able to embezzle large sums from such checks before discovery. Consequently it is recommended that employees be allowed in the mail room on a need basis only and that all others be kept out by supervision.

Cafeteria or Lunch Room

Many companies provide free or low-cost lunches as an employee benefit. In an industrial area where restaurants are not available, this can be very helpful for employee morale. Retailers may allow discounts to employees who purchase food or beverages at the company lunch counter or soda fountain.

It is not unusual for employees to become involved in the petty fraud of allowing friends or members of their immediate families to use these food privileges. While the losses involved in these situations are probably not great, every effort should be made to discourage this kind of operation. Employees sometimes move from deceptions of this kind to other anticompany activities, eventually participating in merchandise or money theft.

It is suggested that rules against this type of activity be clearly set out in the company manual and that facilities be spot-checked from time to time.

Accountability for Career Apparel

Many employees are expected to wear uniforms or clothing items that are readily identifiable with their jobs. The concept of career apparel seems to be gaining acceptance, and insurance companies, banks, and public agencies are now providing work clothes for employees. The furnishing of apparel at least partially at company expense is an increasingly popular benefit for employees.

Many firms absorb the original cost of these clothes, while others divide the cost with employees. In some instances maintenance is the responsibility of the employee, while in others the companies collect the clothing and send it out for laundry service. Garments are charged out to the individual employee when they are issued, but accountability for career apparel frequently becomes lost. Few companies demand a return of the garments issued in the event the employee quits, and most cannot accurately tell how many changes of clothing the employee should be held responsible for.

Replacement costs for uniforms and garments can represent a considerable outlay. The practice of employees discarding clothing items that still have considerable value can usually be controlled if one employee is given specific responsibility to account for garments, and a new or clean item is issued only when it is exchanged for an old or soiled one.

It is also recommended that the personnel file of each employee reflect the numbers and kinds of garments issued to him or her. When a termination interview is conducted, the interviewer should obtain all outstanding uniforms.

The Company Gasoline Pump

Losses experienced at the company gasoline pump in many cases became more critical with the development of the nationwide energy shortage, which brought greater temptation for employee misuse.

Many companies utilize a written log of some type for issuing gasoline by vehicle number for cost accounting purposes. This may be satisfactory if the pump is locked at night and it remains within the view of a supervisor during working hours. Frequently, however, the total fuel recorded as being pumped will be less than the actual amount used, as indicated at the end of the accounting period.

If losses are consistently found in this activity, consideration should be given to a more sophisticated dispensing system. One kind of pump cannot be activated until a special key is inserted, along with a specially printed ticket. If these tickets are numerically controlled and issued, proper accountability should result.

One category of facility subject to employee misuse which has only been touched on is the office. The possibilities of loss through employee misappropriations of office supplies, petty cash, company checks, and so on are discussed in the following chapter, along with other evidences of employee misconduct in the office.

9

Business Office Problems, Employee Shortages, and Bonding

THE BUSINESS OFFICE yields fertile ground for employee misconduct. Readily available office supplies and petty cash funds provide
easy opportunity for employees to help themselves at company
expense. Some office employees also have access to valuables in
safe deposit boxes or to incoming company payments.

Controlling Office Supplies

Pilferage of office supplies and materials can be a continuing
loss problem unless management takes steps to control this activity. While individual amounts may be small, the continuing
buildup can be serious.

Many of the articles that workers take home from the office
have little individual value, and the company may buy them in
huge quantities. But undiscovered theft often tends to be habit
forming. The employee who appropriates a few blank envelopes
to pay his utility bills may thereafter take home a surplus office
typewriter to catch up on his personal correspondence. If there

is no immediate inquiry about the office machine, it may remain at his home indefinitely. It is difficult to know where to draw the line, but after a time "borrowing for keeps" must be regarded as plain dishonesty, regardless of the original intent.

Honest employees are frequently aware of thefts occurring in their department but say nothing to co-workers who are involved. They have chosen to ignore the fact that with rising costs and competition, an accumulation of small thefts can affect the company's profit. Nationally, the losses due to employees who take items that may be useful runs into millions of dollars. Workers who ignore this problem are hurting themselves, as at least part of this money could have gone into employee benefits or higher salaries.

Company attitudes towards pilferage are often indicative of the problem. When the father of a grade school pupil called the school to complain that his son's classmates consistently took pencils and school supplies, he maintained that the cost was not important. "It is the principle of the thing," he said. "I can always supply my son with pencils from my office."

When thinking of this kind is prevalent among employees, it is not surprising that the firm has problems with waste and loss of office supplies. A favorable employee attitude can be cultivated partly by management appeal to the inherent honesty of individuals. It is also helpful to point out that loss prevention can be a factor in the profit structure, the success of which can have direct benefits for the employee.

There are a number of systems for company control of office supply distribution. Some firms maintain supplies in a locked drawer or cabinet located in a central stockroom. Company regulations permit department and staff secretaries to obtain needed items once a week by use of a requisition form, which allows supervision to make regular reviews of requests. A procedure of this kind also eliminates the problem created by allowing everyone in the office to have access to company materials. Free opportunity is often a factor in encouraging pilferage.

Another system that has been successful is to allow each employee to requisition needed supplies on a form at a specific time each day. Under this system, approval by supervision is not required, as the quantities requisitioned by each employee are retained on file. If an occasional check of usage is made by management, it will be apparent when requests exceed the need of individuals.

Petty Cash Funds

Almost every office has a petty cash fund for minor, day-to-day outlays. The amount of money in the petty cash fund varies considerably from company to company. Some funds are nominal, while others may contain a sufficient sum to tempt an outside holdup man. Most petty cash losses, however, originate inside the organization.

A slogan in the comptroller's office of a major New York corporation expresses the philosophy that:

There Is No Such Thing as Petty Cash!

If this slogan is observed, monetary losses from petty cash funds can usually be eliminated.

Control should begin with the establishment of a specific fund administered by a designated employee. When the custodian of the fund is absent, accountability should be continued by an alternate employee. The fund should, of course, be sufficiently large to handle day-to-day requirements without exposing unnecessary cash to the possibility of loss.

It is suggested that no disbursements be made from this fund without an accompanying voucher. The voucher should be approved by a responsible official and signed by the individual receiving the cash. The possibility of altered vouchers can be reduced by using permanent ink or a typewriter in their preparation. Amounts should be written out in full (such as "fifteen dollars") rather than in figures, which are easily alterable.

It is desirable for a responsible member of management other than the employee in charge of the fund to examine individual vouchers for indications of alteration or other fraud. Each of the vouchers should be canceled at that time by use of a perforation device or a rubber stamp that cannot be easily erased. A good accounting control requires unannounced audits of vouchers in the petty cash fund and balancing of the account by a responsible official.

The amount of money in the petty cash fund is usually entered in the general ledger. The fund can be replenished by drawing a check for the total amount of all the paid vouchers on hand.

Borrowing from Petty Cash

Some firms, with or without management approval, permit employees to borrow small sums from the petty cash fund for emergencies. The possibilities of abuse of this practice are self-evident, and it should be prohibited by company rule.

A bookkeeper in an Arizona drug company who frequently ran short of cash before payday got in the habit of borrowing $10 from petty cash and repaying it on payday. The bookkeeper always left an IOU acknowledging that he had taken the money. After he had been making these small extractions for several months, the office manager found out and informed the bookkeeper that this activity had to cease immediately.

Eventually, the bookkeeper again removed money from the petty cash, but this time he made up some receipts that showed nonexistent office expenditures. When an auditor went over the account it was discovered that the receipts had been falsified, and the bookkeeper was discharged. A claim was made by the drug company for reimbursement on the employee's bond, in the amount of $1,200. The bonding company answered that "The bookkeeper regularly took money from petty cash, and your manager knew about it. We cannot be responsible for thefts by an employee after you have found out he was dishonest." Management countered by claiming that the bookkeeper had not really been dishonest when he left an IOU and repaid the money.

When the matter came to trial, the court pointed out that "There was no attempt at concealment of these personal draws and later repayment. Under these circumstances, we cannot say that the company should have recognized these acts as dishonest, if dishonest they in fact were." The court held that the bookkeeper's extractions of cash which were subsequently repaid were not sufficient to be regarded as dishonesty. Accordingly, the bonding company was not allowed to claim prior dishonesty as an excuse and was ordered to pay $1,200.

The drug company recovered its funds, however, only after a long, costly lawsuit, even though the employee had been bonded. Instances of this kind point up the desirability of advising employees that petty cash is only for business use and money can never be borrowed from the fund. It is recommended that employees be put on notice that they are subject to discharge if they use petty cash for any nonbusiness purpose.

Forcing Employees to Make Good on Cash Shortages

At the time salespeople were hired, an Indiana department store required them to sign a promise to pay for any shortages on their cash registers. A complaint concerning this agreement was filed with the U.S. Department of Labor, and eventually the U.S. Court of Appeals held that this agreement was illegal. The reasoning of the court was that if the arrangement was enforced, some employees would receive less than the minimum legal wage.

The department store argued that the reimbursement would be a valid debt and not wages. Also, the store claimed that unless an employee could be held responsible for shortages, clerks would feel they could steal without much risk of punishment.

The court pointed out that the employer's agreement was compulsory in nature and that under it the employee might be forced to pay, whether or not he was at fault regarding the shortage. The court indicated that the agreement would have been valid if it had required repayment of any money that was misappropriated or taken by the clerk.

Negotiable Securities in Safe Deposit Boxes

Negotiable stocks or securities are maintained by some companies in safe deposit boxes at nearby banks. In such cases it is recommended that the corporate attorney take the precaution of drawing up a resolution which limits entry to the deposit box to a few key employees. It is advisable to file signatures of these authorized persons with the bank and to obtain a written confirmation that the bank will be liable unless two of them are present at the time access is granted. It is also suggested that written instructions be issued specifically naming those officials who have authority to sell or negotiate such securities.

In the usual situation of this kind, the value of the stocks in the safe deposit box may be far in excess of the limits for which officials are bonded. To give the company protection, it may be desirable to obtain a schedule position bond for those who have access to these securities. This type of bond provides security not furnished by the regular company bond covering all employees.

A flowchart of an approved procedure for selling or negotiating company stocks held in a deposit box is presented in Figure 2.

FIGURE 2
Procedure for Selling Negotiable Securities in Deposit Box

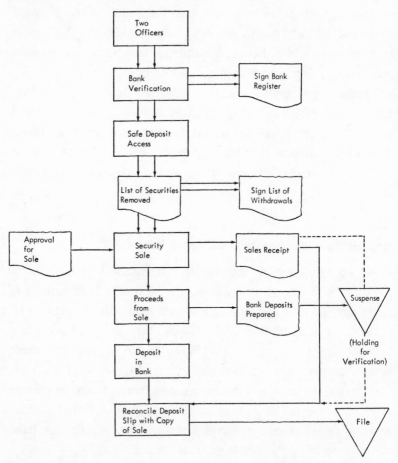

Endorsing Checks to Discourage Embezzlement

The possibilities of embezzlement are always present when a company receives revenue in the mails, as was noted in the preceding chapter. A system of restrictive endorsements on all incoming checks will help to prevent such losses.

A Texas dental supply company received considerable income from mail-order accounts. As checks were received, the customers were given credit and the checks were routed to a clerical employee who had responsibility for making up bank deposits.

Each of these checks was stamped with the firms' name, but when the clerical employee held one of the checks out of the deposit and asked the bank to cash it for her, the bank complied. Concluding that this was an easy way to get money, she repeated this scheme 35 times in the next six months. When the firms' accountants found that all incoming checks had not been deposited, they directed responsibility toward the clerk, who eventually admitted her embezzlements. She was not bonded, and she had no funds that could be used for restitution.

Claiming that the bank had no right to cash such checks and give to the employee, the firm filed suit against the bank. The court felt that the firm's name on the rubber stamp constituted a blank endorsement which have the bank the right to cash the checks and give the money to whoever presented the check for payment.

The dental supply company would have been protected had it placed a restrictive endorsement on the incoming checks. The endorsement should have read for deposit to the account of that company or "For Deposit Only." With an endorsement of this kind, the bank would have been liable had they cashed the checks or given the proceeds to an employee of the dental firm.[1]

Bonding Employees

Many companies regard it as prudent to bond employees who have access to large amounts of cash or property that could be easily carried away and sold. The policy of these firms is that if an applicant has difficulty in obtaining a fidelity bond, he or she will not be offered a job. A more troublesome situation arises when the person refused a bond is already on the company payroll or when an existing bond is canceled.

A salesman for an importer of luxury items was arrested as

---

[1] *Palmer and Ray Dental Supply of Abilene, Inc.* v. *First National Bank of Abilene*, 477 SW 2d 954.

a shoplifter by the security guard at a department store. The salesman claimed that he had absentmindedly placed an article in his pocket and forgotten to pay for it as he left the store. He was released after identifying himself and his employer and after paying for it.

The terms of the company surety bond required that the bonding firm be advised of any arrest, and the salesman's employer followed this stipulation. The salesman's bond was canceled immediately thereafter, and he was discharged from his job. He then appealed to arbitration through his labor union representative.

The arbitrator ruled that the salesman should be reinstated. This result appears to be questionable logic, as it was the salesman himself who deprived the company of the ability to obtain protection on him. The arbitrator seemed to go out of his way in ordering reinstatement on the basis of the salesman's insistence that he had overlooked the item in his pocket and did not actually intend to steal it.

The arbitrator did, however, order some protection for the company. The salesman was instructed to post cash in the amount of $1,000 with his employer in the event he could not obtain a bond, and this sum was to be retained in escrow.

In many instances, a burglary insurance policy taken out by the company may not allow recovery in the event of employee involvement. There is a difference of opinion on this by the courts, however. Some states do allow the policyholder to recover from the insurance company, while in other areas the insurer is allowed to reject the claim.[2]

If management wants to obtain protection against both outside burglary and employee crime of the same kind, it may be advisable to obtain employee fidelity bonds as well as burglary insurance.

---

[2] *Century Indemnity Co.* v. *Schmick,* 88 NW 2d 622; *C&H Plumbing and Heating, Inc.* v. *Employers Mutual Casualty Co,* 287 A2d 238.

10

The Insubordinate Employee

EMPLOYEE insubordination can have its roots in disloyalty or disinterest, although it is seldom dishonest in a legal sense. The
alienated employee becomes openly insubordinate when he lets
his feelings get the better of him. His rebellion may take many
forms: abusive language to management, antagonizing customers,
refusing to work ordered overtime, or slowdowns and work
stoppages.

Not only does the discontented worker involved in an incident
of insubordination delay his own production, he slows down the
output of other employees, who tend to congregate around any
disruption. More time is lost in gossiping about the incident, and
morale for the entire operation declines as workers question
whether the disobedient employee was justified and, if so, whether
they should do likewise in response to their individual complaints.

How does a manager or supervisor prevent the insubordinate
worker from creating such a costly disturbance? The obvious
answer is to make the worker happy in the first place, so any
expression of disaffection does not come to the surface. Of course,

this is often not possible. Many people let their anger build up inside without expressing it until they reach a breaking point where temper displays cannot be stopped. Managers and supervisors often are too busy—or, unfortunately, too imperceptive—to give proper attention to legitimate complaints.

This chapter deals with the practical aspects of what to do after the blowup has taken place. The need for managers and supervisors to uncover and understand workers' complaints before they turn to insubordination is recognized.

Abusive Language

When an employee uses abusive language toward management, a disruption of production is likely to occur, and there may be serious consequences in the relationship between employer and employee. Accordingly, management has always been justified in discharging an employee when a situation of this kind arises.

Even if the employee who verbally abuses management is also a union representative, that fact does not always justify verbal abuse. In the event a union representative does not approve of a move made by management, ordinarily he should resort to the labor-management grievance machinery that has been set up. However, there may be an exception to the rule that employees are subject to discharge for cursing or verbally abusing management. It has become a part of the collective bargaining tradition for both sides to engage in theatrics, name calling, or strong accusations. While this may not be admirable behavior, it has become an accepted part of the bargaining (but not the grievance) procedure.

In one instance, a union official was suspended by his company for accusing members of management of engaging in theft of employee benefits *during a grievance procedure*. The union man requested arbitration to remove the suspension. The arbitration board stated that they did not approve of the union representative's irresponsible language, but the company's discipline was not justified. The board also pointed out, however, that identical language by the union officer would be just cause for discipline if it had been used during the course of a work assignment.

In recent years concern for the right of free speech has been expressed in all levels of society. Employees who bring "hate literature" into industrial plants, commercial establishments, or business offices, or who speak out in favor of private causes, may cite this right. The courts are in agreement that there is no absolute right to speak out at any time and any place without some limitations.

In one instance, an employee brought into the production area of a plant a document which was a bitter denunciation of management and which made a number of charges against the company that were completely false. In addition, the employee circulating this document accused the company union of neglecting employee rights and of being completely dominated by management. As might be anticipated, the firm discharged this employee, who advised the union that the only way to disprove the claim of management domination was to press a grievance.

In the hearing that resulted, the company argued that discharge did not deprive the worker of any right. The firm's spokesman did not dispute an individual's basic right to freedom of speech, pointing out that there was nothing to stop a worker from attacking the company verbally while off the premises. But he maintained that no employee has a right to circulate libelous material within the company's own plant.

The labor arbitrator stated that the employee had become involved in a reckless disregard for the truth. If such action were allowed on company property, the effect would be to foster mistrust and discord in the plant. The arbitrator also said that management has the right to protect itself against unjust attacks and that a worker cannot hold management up to hatred on a company bulletin board, by placards, cartoons, graffiti, or otherwise.[1]

Refusal to Work

Outright refusal by a worker to do a requested task would seem to be grounds for dismissal or suspension, but this is not always the case. An employee who ordinarily does one routine job may refuse to do a more strenuous piece of work if at the time he truthfully explains a physical weakness which prevents such labor. Arbitrators have held that it is up to the supervisor to find out why such a task is refused before disciplinary action is taken.

One female worker neglected to tell her foreman why she did not do a physically harder job she had been given, and she was fired. While her dismissal was later reversed by the arbitrator, she still lost her back pay. The reason given was that she should have told her supervisor of her disabling condition rather than allowing him to think she was blatantly insubordinate.

A machine worker who was afraid to help the repairman fix his machine as he had been told to do was suspended. Because the supervisor did not find out the reason for the worker's refusal to help the repairman before he took disciplinary action, an arbitrator had the man reinstated. Although the foreman may not have considered that there was a potential for a safety hazard if the worker helped the repairman, in the opinion of the worker there was such a hazard. His prudence was rewarded. If the foreman had looked into the reason for the man's reluctance, another assistant could have been procured temporarily while the worker was assigned to a different task.

Refusal to work outside of one's craft is no justification for walking off the job if the supervisor feels that such an assignment

---

[1] In re *Great Lakes Steel Corporation and United Steelworkers of America, Local 1299,* Case No. 72–B–329, Grievance No. 1429–M, May 14, 1973, 60 LA 860.

is reasonably associated with the worker's primary job description. At any rate, the correct thing for the worker to do would be to comply with the request and then question it within the grievance framework, rather than taking action on his own.

In many situations involving refusal to work an apology may be enough to correct the situation. Demanding a public apology from an insubordinate employee usually does not stand well with labor arbitrators, however. In most cases of insubordination where management's feelings are hurt, a stronger penalty is usually supported by arbitrators. A published apology from the worker on the company bulletin board is ordinarily overturned in the worker's favor.

Refusal to Work Overtime

An employee's refusal to work ordered overtime beyond his or her regular shift is often held as a punishable infraction by management, regardless of the circumstances. In some cases, however, imposing penalties for this is open to question. Refusal to work overtime points out that not all people are motivated to work entirely for money. Many prefer to have the same amount of time off each week and are disinterested in receiving a larger paycheck for working a few more hours.

Turning down such assignments is justified when notice is given to the employer long enough in advance so that another worker can be given the overtime. In declining overtime, a reasonable excuse for this action must be provided by the worker. *Constant* refusal to work ordered overtime can justify suspension or dismissal.

While it may seem that arbitrators are trying to do away with management's right to schedule overtime, this is definitely not the case. However, where there is no union contract to the contrary and the organization is on a five-day, 40-hour week, the right of employees to turn down overtime is usually upheld. It is a good idea to specify in agreements with unions when ordered overtime must be worked.

While a reasonable excuse must always be given for refusing overtime, management must also have a reasonable need for requesting an individual to work overtime. This latter rule is often interpreted as meaning that the overtime must be ordered due to unforeseen circumstances or an emergency. A skilled worker could correctly refuse unscheduled overtime which involved menial tasks when there are many semiskilled employees available for the extra work.

Antagonizing Customers

Few labor arbitration cases exist where a former employee seeks reinstatement after being discharged for antagonizing a customer. This is largely due to the hopelessness of the worker for recourse in such situations.

However, there is the case of the service representative who was injured while fixing a customer's appliance. When the repairman decided to sue the customer for negligence, management instructed him to discontinue the litigation because the customer was threatening to take his business to a competitor. The service representative was fired upon his refusal to drop the lawsuit. The arbitrator reinstated the service representative in his job.

Just as there is legislation to protect a worker from any revenge by his supervisor when the former brings suit evolving from the work relationship, one can exercise his legal rights without losing his job. The same holds true when management states that a worker is guilty of wrongdoing. The worker can bring a slander suit without fear of sacrificing his job if it is proven that he actually did no wrong and thereby suffered damage from his employer's accusations.

Boycotting the Company Product

As a part of management's expectations of loyalty from employees, it is often expected that the company product will be purchased or used by the employees. It is also expected that complaining against the company will be restricted to employee circles and that the company product will not be downgraded or ridiculed to outsiders.

In one case of this nature, a company employee was heard to brag that he never bought the company's product and that he had exerted influence on many other individuals not to utilize the product either. Boasting that he was a union officer and there would be no peace for the company so long as he was there, he threatened to foul up the company product and have all union members do likewise unless the company decided not to remove one of the Coke machines in the plant.

This employee was immediately discharged for threatening a boycott. A labor arbitrator upheld this discharge, pointing out that as a union official as well as an employee this man had an obligation to make certain that the labor agreement with the company was upheld. Pressure tactics against the company could not be used.[2]

Another case involved a Ford automobile dealer who had a service employee who purchased a new Rambler, drove it to work, and parked it on the company lot. After a discussion of company loyalty, the worker was discharged. A grievance was filed, and the case came to arbitration.

In seeking to defend the discharge, the Ford dealer pointed out that he would have a more difficult time persuading customers to buy Fords if his own employees favored the products of competitors. The man who had been discharged argued that everyone

---

[2] *Sinclair Oil and Gas Company, Plant No. 25(Silsbee, Tex.)* and *Oil, Chemical and Atomic Workers International Union*, FMCS File No. 63A–75, October 8, 1962, 39 LA 508.

has a right to buy the product he wants. He also pointed out that the car was jointly owned with his wife, and she favored the Rambler.

The arbitrator held in favor of the discharged employee, awarding him his back wages. He was not reinstated, since he had obtained another job in the interval. The arbitrator pointed out that an employee is not required to spend his money where he earns it. Neither is a service employee required to favor the kind of automobiles he works on.[3]

The point was not made here that the use of a competitor's product can have a very disturbing influence on other employees and would be objectionable for that reason. Whether this argument would have influenced a different decision is a matter of conjecture.

Does the Punishment Fit the Crime?

Special care must be exercised in disciplining insubordinate employees. Whether or not the rebellious worker is represented by a labor union, any punishment must be meted out fairly, and all infractions should be carefully documented. In the case of union representation, two further considerations must be given.

First, management must determine whether certain actions are stipulated under the covenants signed with unions. Many labor-management contracts state that while strikes are permissible if sponsored by the union, isolated walkouts, work stoppages, sick-ins, or slowdowns are not allowed. Under agreements of this nature, union members who purposely engage in an illegal slow-down, for example in protest of a plant's new higher production incentive rates, can be suspended. If the established grievance pro-

---

[3] In re *Paul Swanson* (Los Gatos, Calif.) *and International Association of Machinists, Industrial District Lodge No. 93*, March 10, 1961, 36 LA 305.

cedures are followed and it comes to arbitration, management's action is usually sustained in such a case.

Second, it is important to keep careful records of all incidences of poor performance or insubordination. In the case of a work stoppage protesting higher incentive rates, management was able to go back to the files of each of the workers who had walked off the job and produce histories of deficient output that had been recorded before the initiation of the new program. Each employee had previously been reprimanded for inadequate production. While the union contract in this case permitted discharge for walkouts, management selected the lesser chastisement of suspension. This action was upheld when the question was eventually arbitrated.

In cases of slowdowns and walkouts, management too often gives rash punishments without considering individual differences. These are later set aside in arbitration because little documentation of earlier poor conduct has been kept by the employer, and unions usually stress the reduction of penalties for workers who previously have had good records. It works the other way as well. A poor record can be used by management as the basis for stronger corrective measures.

Dissimilar punishment of two workers for the same offense will sometimes be sustained. When proof can be produced to verify that one worker has been reprimanded for earlier disobedience and no evidence of this nature can be brought against another employee, the former can be more severely punished than the latter. Then, too, the actions of a shop steward, because he is a union representative who must follow certain contractual obligations and serve as an example of good conduct, leave him open to more severe treatment than that accorded fellow union members. However, it is not open hunting season on shop stewards. Unless the union contract calls for preventative action by the steward in the case of an illegal slowdown or walkout, he can vindicate himself by taking no steps, either for or against the protest. Under an agreement where the steward is required to step in, he can protect himself if he engages in the disturbance after he has conscientiously tried to dissuade co-workers from it. In either of these cases, the shop steward can be punished, but no more than other participants.

Both management and labor are taking positive steps in the areas of discipline. Management is moving away from punishment for the sake of vengeance, while unions are discouraging histrionics by shop stewards. Unions are trying to introduce a greater degree of professionalism in the grievance procedure because they realize that a hot-headed act by a single representative of organized labor can destroy goodwill with management. This can impede future betterment of working conditions and place the membership in a position where it does not want to be. Management is looking beyond immediate discipline and finding merit in fair-minded treatment of employee complaints to discourage insubordination before it happens. This mutuality of interest should assure smoother operations in the future.

11

Disclosure of Trade Secrets

EVEN THOUGH one can spend a lifetime in business without ever encountering industrial espionage, it would be naive to believe it cannot be the cause of serious business losses. The extent of corporate espionage has been estimated by some as costing U.S. firms many billions of dollars per year, while others say that such figures are greatly exaggerated. The gravity of the problem is attested to by the investigative agencies that have been developed to cope with industrial espionage and provide protective countermeasures.

The pervasiveness of industrial espionage can be indicated by the regularity with which incidents come to light indicating that company secrets are being used by competitors or have even become common knowledge in the trade. Usually, a business does not know it has been victimized until it is too late.

The industrial spy has innumerable methods for gathering secret information. He may gain entry into the premises by posing as a government or state inspector checking on plant safety, fire protection equipment, or plumbing installations. A microphone could be planted in the office of a key executive, or telephones could be tapped. An industrial spy can gain access to almost any area by posing, for example, as a new employee, an elevator technician, or a worker in the janitorial service. Most of the techniques and rules of the corporate spy can be circumvented if company security programs are properly carried out.

While the cloak and dagger techniques of the professional corporate spy cannot be disregarded, more frequently it is the disloyalty or disaffection of employees or ex-employees that is involved. In many cases, the culprit is not a spy in the real sense of the word but a company insider, a disgruntled employee, or someone hard-pressed for cash.

Legitimate Sources of Competitive Information

There are many ways in which information about competitive firms can be gathered in a legitimate way. In some industries it is the practice for company executives or engineers to make direct contacts with acquaintances in other companies. In the steel industry, for example, mutual friends in different firms may pass on test results of advances in processes and alloys. In other businesses, an executive may request a catalog and specific test data on a competitor's products.

Businesses which are cooperative in the exchange of competitive information believe that this approach works to the advantage of everyone in the industry. Cooperation results in higher product standards, an accelerated rate of technological development, and increased public respect for the entire industry. But in some industries the market is not broad enough for all to share equally. Since companies are in business to make money, they understandably want to protect the unusual techniques or capacities that give them an advantage. A company that has put out funds for research and development should reap the benefits of such a program.

Some companies inadvertently disclose their secrets through "ego displays" by executives or technical experts—individuals bent on demonstrating their ability to their counterparts in rival companies. Some of this may be nothing more than evidence of pride. In some instances, the professional interests of scientists and technicians seem to exceed company loyalty. The desire for improvement and product development may motivate these individuals, regardless of the firms they work for.

It is not unusual for firms to send expert employees to trade shows where they can examine, sketch, or photograph any product that is put on general display. This is one of the risks the manufacturer takes in presenting his merchandise for the examination of buyers.

If most of the companies in an industry rely on the same sources of supply, information can be disclosed by contacts with these suppliers. In an effort to improve his position with a buyer, a supplier may furnish confidential details he has observed in another firm's operation. Business consultants also can furnish information as to the activities of other firms with which they have been in contact.

Keeping Trade Secrets Secret

A trade secret is any device, method, or formula with a commercial value that is known to the manufacturer who uses it but not to his competitors. In the case of *Victor Chemical Works* v. *Iliff,*[1] the court defined a trade secret as "a plan or process, tool, mechanism, or compound known only to its owner and those of his employees to whom it is necessary to confide it."

A good number of firms utilize trade secrets in manufacturing or preparing their product. Because of the ease with which employees can take secrets from job to job, these firms would be

---

[1] *Victor Chemical Works* v. *Iliff et al.,* 132 NE 806; 299 Ill 532.

hard-pressed to protect themselves without some help from the courts.

A patent is the standard legal device for protecting the rights of the person who works out an invention. It gives a production monopoly to the patent holder. Only certain things are patentable under the strict requirements of the federal patent laws, however. Because drawings and descriptive papers must be submitted to obtain a patent, secret features are unavoidably revealed in the process.

In most instances, a patent is issued for a mechanical device. A trade secret is something the holder wants to retain as a secret. It may be nothing more than expertise in using the device or a method for mixing ingredients, joining materials together, or combining chemicals in a certain ratio.

The British and American courts have always taken the approach that if a firm can work out an unusual product, it is entitled to keep its methods secret. A competitor has every right to buy the finished product, take it into his laboratory, and analyze it in every way possible. If he can discover a way to duplicate the product or improve on it through his own efforts, his product can be placed on the market. But there are some restrictions the courts will enforce. A competitor cannot gain the secret from an employee who has been given the responsibility of guarding confidential knowledge. Nor can the competitor bribe an employee to reveal a trade secret or obtain it through a spy planted inside the business.

The courts will consistently give protection by granting an injunction against a defecting employee who takes a trade secret to his new job or against a competitor who obtains the secret unfairly. If the owner is to receive this protection, however, he must demonstrate to the court that he had taken affirmative steps to retain the matter as a secret. There are several methods by which secrecy can be achieved:

1. Secret formulas or methods should be kept in a safe or under lock and key when not being used.
2. Any documents regarding the secret should be marked "secret," "confidential," or with some designation that will put employees on notice.
3. Coded symbols or language should be used where practical to protect the secret material or its components.
4. Access should be restricted on a "job need" basis and permitted only in those areas of the plant or office where the secret is used.
5. A badge or pass system may be used to further limit access.
6. In some instances the use of security guards or protective devices may be appropriate.
7. When employees are hired, an agreement should be obtained in writing whereby they promise to protect the confidential nature of the company's trade secrets as a condition of employment.
8. When employees sever their connections with the company, they should be reminded of their responsibilities and obligations to protect trade secrets.

What Is the Life of a Trade-Secret?

There is no limit as to how long a trade secret can be retained as confidential. The legal limits imposed by the statute of limitations do not apply. It remains the property of the originator until it is no longer secret or no longer used. He is entitled to protection as long as he remains in business.

Taking a Trade Secret to the Competition

It is a legal wrong for a departing employee to bring a trade secret to his new employer. The company that holds the secret is not required to have a written agreement to this effect with those employees who work with confidential matters, although a written agreement is better than a verbal admonition.

The defense claim most frequently made when an employer brings suit for theft of a trade secret is that it had become known to a number of persons and was therefore no longer a secret. But disclosure to any number of employees does not invalidate the secret nature of the material. If it is found necessary for many different employees to work with secret material or processes, disclosure en masse does not negate its confidential quality, as long as management tries to keep it secret.

There are some well-known examples, such as that of Coca-Cola, where the owner has managed to restrict a secret formula to very few persons, but this is not a requirement laid down by the courts. There also is no requirement that the trade secret be an involved or complicated device, process, or formula. It can be quite simple and easily duplicated, so long as it is secret and it produces an unusual result.

If suit is brought against a defecting employee, the courts usually take the approach that it is up to him to prove that the secret had already leaked out. Proving that it has been disclosed to many other workers is not sufficient. It must either have been disclosed to outsiders or discovered independently and then used rather commonly in the trade.

A limitation is also placed on the employer. He cannot claim everything he does in his business is a trade secret. He must isolate a specific device, method, or formula and take steps to see that it is treated as secret.

An automobile window manufacturer hired away two experienced glass workers from a competitor. These two workers had neither employment contracts nor high positions with their first employer. Therefore, there was no legal basis for the court to forbid them to work for the second employer. To have done so would "seriously impinge on their freedom of choice as to work and trade."

The original employer of the two workers filed suit against the second company, claiming that the workers had brought stolen trade secrets to their new firm. This was emphatically denied by the second employer, who introduced convincing testimony to point out that:

1. The first company had not secured promises from the two workers to protect trade secrets at the time they were hired or at any later time.
2. The first company had no real program of any kind to protect secrets. In fact, visitors to the plant were frequently taken on tours and allowed to handle and inspect everything that was being made.

The court agreed and pointed out that trade secrets may be entrusted to even the lowest paid employee of a company, but if management fails to make the effort to treat such matters as confidential, they will not be protected against competition.[2]

Proving Trade Secret Thefts by Tape-Recorded Admissions

A chemist who had worked with production secrets at a toy factory for a number of years was lured away by a competing firm. The company to which the chemist moved then began to make products that seemed to be almost identical with those sold by the original employer.

The president of the first company invited the chemist over for a talk and managed to obtain some verbal admissions of trade secret abuse. This conversation was recorded on a concealed tape recorder in the president's desk. A lawsuit was then filed against the chemist and the concern to which he had defected.

---

[2] *Flexo Glass Corp.* v. *Protective Glass Co.,* 322 F Supp 854.

When this matter came to trial, the tape recording was allowed in evidence by the court, although the chemist and his attorney protested strongly against the use of the secret recording. The judge hearing this matter awarded money damages to the first company and issued an injunction forbidding the chemist from disclosing any further techniques or secrets to his present employer.

In allowing the tape to be used as evidence, the court said that the party offering the tape must prove:

1.   That the tape had not been tampered with, edited, or altered.
2.   That the tape was true and complete.
3.   That the voices of the persons engaged in the conversation were identified by testimony of witnesses.

The use of the tape recorder is usually quite different from the situation in which a damaging telephone call is recorded. There are a number of legal restrictions that may come into play if a telephone conversation is recorded without the prior knowledge and approval of both parties to the conversation. Legal advice should be obtained on this issue, as the recording involving the telephone may be a criminal violation.

In most jurisdictions the best way to collect evidence in this situation is to have a third party listen in on an extension telephone. Even this arrangement is against the law in some locations, however.

Reconstructing Secrets by Research and Development

Chemical and Engineering specialists in a firm's research and development department are frequently assigned to analyze items sold by competitors, as noted above. This kind of activity is not considered to be illegal by the courts. These researchers may also switch from company to company and continue to evaluate competitive merchandise. A man's analytical ability in breaking down a competitor's product is considered a skill by the courts. It is not regarded as being a violation of trade secrets.[3]

Protecting Executive Salary Scales against Disclosure

An executive's salary information is not classified as a trade secret by the court. The executive is free to reveal his own salary in seeking another position if he so desires, but this disclosure should not be extended to include the pay of other officials or employees in his company.

It is altogether different for a person seeking a better job to disclose a confidential salary list for use in a raid on his present or past employer's key personnel. The courts will award damages to a company whose salary lists were wrongfully revealed if employees are lured away as a result of this disclosure.[4]

[3] *Buckingham Chemical Company* v. *Rolland,* 160 A 2d 430.
[4] *Bancroft-Whitney Company* v. *Glen,* 411 P2d 921.

12

Moonlighting

SEVERAL GENERATIONS ago, the average American employee supplemented his income by working a garden plot or living on a small farm. There was no conflict between home chores and the work performed on the job. When people changed from this semi-rural kind of living to urban surroundings, many workers had to seek out other ways to supplement their incomes. The shorter work week also left employees with more free time. As a consequence, moonlighting has become an accepted way of life to many people.

Objections to Moonlighting

Many employers strongly oppose moonlighting, however. In the first place, any additional work may result in loss of efficiency on the regular job, especially if the worker puts in too many hours on the outside and does not remain physically and mentally fit. What happens, of course, is that the second job decreases the value of the worker's services on the first one.

In addition, the job performed while moonlighting is sometimes one that would otherwise have been performed by the worker's own company. In instances of this kind it is not surprising that management resents being deprived of business.

As a practical matter it will also be found with some frequency that the moonlighter makes use of the tools, facilities, and supplies of his regular employer. He may simply "appropriate" the parts he uses in making repairs, or he may shorten the life of his regular employer's machinery and equipment.

There is another objection to holding a second job that can be even more serious. Since moonlighting frequently involves the same skills and trade techniques as the employee's regular work, the secondary job is often in the same line of work, for a competitor of the primary employer. This can lead to the revelation of business secrets, future plans, or marketing intentions. Disclosures of this type can be very costly to the regular employer.

Many firms can and should control or prohibit outside work by their employees. This can be done by advising all individuals on the payroll that they cannot accept any kind of outside work without specific, written approval. A verbal warning of this kind is sufficient to put the employee on notice that he cannot moonlight, but verbal instructions sometimes lead to misunderstandings. It is therefore suggested that the policy against moonlighting be placed in writing and prominently displayed. It should be in terms that clearly prohibit any kind of outside work for another company without approval.

Is Moonlighting Legal?

Clearly, there is nothing illegal in performing personal chores at home after working hours. And, legally, there is no unwritten, implied requirement that an employee must devote 100 percent of his working time to his firm. Moonlighting is not legal in all instances, however.

As a general rule, it is regarded as wrong by the courts to hold a second job that conflicts with the business interest of the worker's own firm. For example, a meat packer could work on a truck farm, but if meat was also butchered there such a job would be in conflict with the interests of his primary job.

The courts have consistently said that no one should be permitted to work *secretly* for a competing company, even though the specific job involved at the outside company is not the kind normally performed by the moonlighting individual. As a specific case, a supervisor at a printing plant took a job with a rival company because he was disappointed in not receiving a promotion to a better job. Through hard work and good performance, the employee soon progressed to a supervisory position at his second place of employment.

When one of the officials of the second firm made a surprise visit to the employee's former company, he found that the employee was moonlighting there as a linotype operator. When questioned about this, the employee pointed out that he had never violated any confidence or used other skills learned on the second job and that he had restricted his moonlighting activities to operating the linotype machine.

The current employer then instructed that there would be no future moonlighting, and a notice was placed on the bulletin board pointing out that a new company rule forbade anyone from engaging in work for a competing or similar company. Employees working for outside firms were instructed to advise the personnel department of the name of the employer and the nature of the duties involved.

Several months later, one of the officials of the second firm again saw the employee working for his old company. He was immediately discharged by his primary employer. It was pointed out that the very fact that an individual works for a competitor suggests divided loyalty. Even if the job assignment while moonlighting for a competitor was nothing other than sweeping up the floor, it would be considered as wrong. The employee had access to a considerable amount of customer specifications and confidential information, and there was always the possibility that he could unwittingly disclose information that would damage his primary employer. This is the reasoning that is consistently followed by the courts and by arbitrators in such situations.

The courts usually also say that the salary paid to an individual who is competing with his own company on the sly must be turned over to the primary employer. This is so even though that employer may not be able to prove that he was actually damaged.

When the Courts Favor Moonlighting

The courts have been very liberal toward employees in interpreting employee contracts. The approach usually taken is that moonlighting will be allowed unless there is a clear company rule to the contrary. It is public policy to favor free employment unless the employer has established the fact that working on a second job will not be permitted and has made this clear to the employee.

In one case a company official was given a written contract by the terms of which he agreed "to devote all of his time, attention, and energy to his duties." This official regularly worked five days a week on an eight-hour basis for his company, but he also worked weekends as a part-time real estate agent, owned an interest in a garage, wrote material for a technical book at home, and traded on the stock market with his own funds.

None of these activities were in direct competition with the employer's business, but a contract dispute resulted. The employer claimed that all this activity added up to moonlighting in violation of the written contract. The court in this case held for the employee, pointing out that the requirement "to devote all of his time, attention, and energy to his duties" referred only to his activities while engaged in his regular work week.

In a somewhat similar case, the official of one firm contracted "to give his full time to the company services." When this contract came into issue in the courts, it was ruled that he was not required to make his talents available to the employer on a 24-hour per day basis, nor even to give "every moment of his waking hours."[1]

As a result of decisions of this kind, management should clearly specify in the employment contract that the worker may not become involved in any outside commercial venture or money-making activity, if this is its intention.

Can Employees Be Forbidden to Moonlight if It Has Been Allowed in the Past?

Disturbed because it was learned that company secrets had been revealed to competitors before new products had left the drawing boards, one major firm immediately posted a written rule to the effect that no employee could work in any capacity for a firm engaged in the sale, manufacture, or design of products similar or related to those of the company.

This notice was quite disturbing to the firm's employees because a number of them had been moonlighting with outside firms for several years. Some of the outside jobs were with competitors of the firm, while others were with suppliers of competing firms. This situation had gone on for so long and had ensnarled so many company employees that the labor union maintained the rule could not be established without prior negotiation.

---

[1] *Johnson* v. *Stoughton Wagon Co.*, 95 NW 394. See also *Terrell* v. *Tool Equipment Sales Co.*, 67 NE 2d 298, 329 Ill. App 183, which holds that similar language did not prohibit outside business connections or attention to personal business.

When this dispute came to arbitration, it was ruled that the company has the right to set out reasonable rules for plant operation. The arbitrator also pointed out that the company could require employees to inform management of all outside jobs held and could immediately prohibit moonlighting with a competing firm. This is basic to the protection of the company and is not a right of employees.[2]

Moonlighting by Outside Sales Employees

Frequently companies do not expect salesmen to work any set number of hours; they are more interested in the results obtained than in an exact accounting of the salesmen's time. On jobs of this nature the salesman may accomplish more by entertainment and contacts at night than by working an 8:00 to 5:00 shift. If the employer wants to make certain that all of the salesman's efforts are for the benefit of the employer, a specific statement to that effect should be incorporated in the employment contract.

In a test case on this issue, a contract dispute arose between a manufacturer and the company salesman assigned to work a specific territory. Needing to supplement his income, the salesman also sold life and fire insurance on the side. Holding that the salesman's side activities were not improper, the court informed the manufacturer that it could very easily have obtained the right to all of the salesman's services by inserting a clause in the employment contract which prohibited outside sales efforts.[3]

Selling on the Job

Almost any good-sized company has full-time employees who sell merchandise on the side. Some of these individuals engage

[2] In re F. E. Myers & Bro. Company (Ashland, Ohio) and *International Association of Machinists, Lodge 1297.* FMCS File No. 64 A/3350, July 31, 1964, 43 LA 338.

[3] *Elliott-Greer Office Supply Co.* v. *Martin,* 54 SW 2d 1068.

in this activity on their own time, usually making door-to-door calls in the neighborhood in which they live. This is, of course, a form of moonlighting on a part-time basis.

Problems do not usually arise until merchandise is offered for sale to fellow employees at work. Then considerable productive time may be lost while the buyer looks at merchandise or catalogs and the seller writes up orders. Female employees frequently offer to sell cosmetics, hosiery, sewing accessories, Christmas cards, and notions. Male employees may come to work equipped with life insurance application forms, shoe catalogs, or other merchandise items.

Experience shows that productive time is lost unless company rules are put into effect prohibiting such sales activity on company time. Some firms advise employees that they have no objection to this kind of activity provided both the buyer and seller are careful to handle these transactions during lunch or break periods.

Newspaper boys, flower vendors, and shoeshine boys are allowed to make daily trips through some facilities. Here again, if too much activity of this kind is permitted, the distractions that result may outweigh the advantages to company employees.

13

Conflict of Interest

CONFLICT OF INTEREST can be the high-level counterpart of trade-secret peddling or moonlighting by rank-and-file employees. Officers, executives, and directors of a company have more inside information available to them than the average stockholder or employee, and much of this information may be confidential. When a highly placed company representative becomes involved in an outside business deal, there is always a possibility that his efforts may be in competition with those of his employer. A conflict of interest is not always self-evident, especially if the outside firm is privately operated by the individual. But if that outside company manages to obtain business that would have otherwise fallen to the company employing the insider, the courts say there is a conflict.

Out of a sense of fairness, the courts consistently hold that a highly placed officer or executive must not take advantage of his own firm. A conflict of interest does not mean a conflict of jobs. A director of a corporation, for example, may not be employed by anyone, but he may have a financial stake in ventures that benefit him personally at the expense of the company he serves as a director.

As a general principle of law, the courts will protect companies against high-level executives or officers who make secret or improper profits by devious dealings. Anyone connected with management as an officer, executive, or director must retain basic loyalty to his firm. This means that he must give his company first call on any business deal that falls in the scope of that firm's interests.

Taking Advantage of Corporate Opportunity

Thus high-level executives, officers, or directors of a corporation are never allowed to interfere with or take advantage of corporate opportunity. In one case, the director of a company learned that his firm was looking for a site for the location of a new plant along a specific freeway in the Long Beach, California, area. The director secretly advised his brother-in-law and furnished money for him to buy up the only available tract that would fit this need. The brother-in-law subsequently sold this land to the corporation at a tremendous markup, secretly splitting the profit with the director.

Eventually the details of this transaction became known, and the corporation sued the profit-minded director. When the matter came to trial, the court said that the director had been disloyal to his trust, and he was forced to give his profits back to the corporation.

In a somewhat similar case the director of a Iowa corporation sold a piece of land to his firm for use as an industrial site. He received almost three times what he had originally paid for the land, and some of the minority stockholders sued the director for a return of profits. In this case, however, the court allowed the director to retain the money. There was nothing secret about the sale, and the director freely disclosed what he had originally paid for the property. He had not bought the land in contemplation of a sale to his company but had obtained it more than 18 years earlier, and all land in that area had increased in value several times over. Independent appraisals of the property made at his request indicated that the sale price was reasonable and fair. In addition, the firm had shopped around for some time without finding a suitable site at a more favorable price.

Ordinarily, no employee or officer of a firm is allowed to profit from doing business with his own company. Executives and officers may become aware of the scarcity of certain items in the course of their duties. They may be able to obtain these items because of personal connections that have nothing to do with their company positions and may then sell them to their company, perhaps turning down a higher profit from competition. These extenuating circumstances are immaterial if the individual makes any personal profit out of such activities. He can be sued by the stockholders for conflict of interest and forced to give up whatever profit he has made.

In such a situation, the company executive or office may have had the best of intentions when he sold scarce materials to his own company. He may even have believed he was doing the company a favor. To be involved in a conflict of interest it is not necessary that he be evasive, secretive, or underhanded. All that is necessary is that he must have profited from a transaction with his own firm.

It could be argued that the executive or officer was not required to spend his personal time and energy in locating scarce materials and that if he had done nothing at all, the firm would have been in a worse position. This is of no consequence, in the viewpoint of the courts. They consistently say that an executive, officer, or director is not allowed to make a profit in dealing with his own firm.

New Business Opportunities

From the statements frequently made by courts, it is apparent that an executive, officer, or director must refrain from competing with his own firm. The legal restrictions go even further, to encompass participation in new business opportunities. If a prospective business is one that would supply an executive's company or an activity that would logically extend the business of the firm, he may be sued if he participates in the new activity.

An executive who wants to protect himself prior to involvement in a new outside business activity should first ask whether his firm wants to take advantage of the opportunity. If the company decides against participation, he is free to avail himself of it.

What this amounts to is that the company must be given the first refusal right. One of the problems is that many firms are so diversified they may decide to go into any potentially profitable sideline at almost any time. This is especially true when firms have surplus funds that must be put to work.

Directors and Competition

A director who is not a company executive or officer may be an exception in conflict of interest cases. State courts have frequently been in dispute as to whether such a director can engage in activities which may be competitive with those of a firm he serves as director. Most of the recent cases have tended to allow such a director to compete.

The reasoning of the courts is that corporations need experienced, knowledgeable directors. A single individual often serves as a director of several corporations simultaneously, and all these companies may profit from his judgment and background. Another thing that has influenced the courts is that the director is usually nonsalaried and must be able to make profits out of his own activities.

The courts usually say that a director is not held to quite the same standards as an executive or officer of the company. As a full-time employee, the officer must always be on the lookout for profitable business deals that are within the scope of the company's policies and capabilities. The director, on the other hand, does not owe all his working time and interests to the firm. He is a leader who guides or controls the company, sets policy, and establishes objectives.

An officer of a company who also serves in the capacity of a director of the firm cannot use the fact that he is a director to escape his noncompete responsibilities as an officer, however. He must allow his company to have first refusal rights at new business opportunities that come to his attention. And it is understood that he must continue to deal openly and fairly with his firm at all times.

Stockholder Approval

When a challenge is made of a business deal between a firm and one of its executives, officers, or directors, the inquiry is usually initiated by a minority stockholder who feels that the majority owners may be taking advantage of other stockholders. An officer or director who wants to make a legitimate business deal with his firm may realize that there are some stockholders who would oppose such a transaction. If a majority of noninvolved stockholders can be brought to vote to approve the transaction, it will be considered legal. In a vote of this kind, the officer or director who wants to make the business deal cannot vote his own stock.

Of course, stockholder approval is dependent on disclosure of all pertinent facts and proof that the deal itself is not fraudulent. A vote of the stockholders cannot authorize an illegal transaction or one that is fraudulent by its own terms. The courts will not support any vote by stockholders that amounts to outright dissipation or waste of the firm's assets. Stockholders also cannot vote approval for any action that is outside the scope of the authority or power given to the company in its legal charter or papers of incorporation.

Resigning from the Company

Most business executives or officers know that they cannot actively compete with their own company. An individual in this position may resign and go into business himself. However, he cannot take advantage of information learned in the scope of his employment to establish his own business. Neither can he apply such information while working for others.

The courts consistently say that if the executive's knowledge of a business opportunity derives from his former company connection, he cannot take advantage of it. To allow a departing executive to use information learned while on the job would be unfair to his previous employer. When a lawsuit results from a situation of this kind, the courts usually say that the individual who resigned must hand over any profits he has made to his former company. The good faith intentions of the competing ex-employee will be considered by the jury in deciding whether a judgment should be rendered against him.

Noncompete Agreements

When one firm buys out another, it is common for the seller to promise not to compete in that business in the future or for a specified number of years. This agreement can be included as one of the provisions of the contract of sale. Agreements of this kind are quite uniformly upheld by the courts.

A written agreement by an employee promising that he will not compete is a different situation from a legal standpoint. A typical noncompete agreement of this type is shown in Figure 3. Statutes and court decisions in some states do not allow these agreements to be enforced against the worker. California and Michigan are among the states that will not permit such agreements.

In most states, however, a noncompete agreement can be enforced against the worker if he receives something of reasonable

FIGURE 3
Typical Noncompete Agreement

THIS AGREEMENT is made and entered into this____day of_____, 19 , by and between_____, hereinafter referred to as "Employer", and _____, hereinafter referred to as "Employee."

In consideration of employment and remuneration to be paid by the Employer to the Employee during such employment, and other valuable considerations received by the Employee, the Employee hereby covenants and agrees to the following:

1. The Employee will devote all of his working time and attention to the Employer's business during the tenure of his employment by the employer.

2. During the tenure of his employment by the Employer and for a period of three (3) years from the date such employment ceases due to resignation from the employment by the Employee or discharge for just cause by the Employer, the Employee will not directly or indirectly, alone or as a member of a partnership, or as an officer, director, stockholder or employee of any corporation, or by or through or as a part of any other entity, tender any service of any value whatsoever, or otherwise engage in any business or other activity (including but not limited to solicitation of Employer's clients) that is competitive with the business conducted by the Employer within three hundred (300) miles of any place wheresoever the Employer, during the effective period of this contract, shall be engaged in the operation of its business.

3. The Employee recognizes and acknowledges that the list of the Employer's clients, as it may exist from time to time, is a valuable, special and unique asset of the Employer's business. The Employee will not, during or after the tenure of his employment, disclose the list of the Employer's clients, or any part thereof, directly or indirectly, to any person, partnership, corporation, or any other entity other than for the benefit of the Employer.

4. The Employee agrees not to divulge, during or after his tenure of employment, any confidential or proprietary information acquired by reason of his employment to any person, partnership, corporation, or any other entity other than as authorized by the Employer.

5. The parties hereto agree that any questions concerning interpretation or enforcement of this contract shall be governed by Florida Law.

THIS AGREEMENT becomes effective this____day of_____, 19__.

WITNESSES: Employee's Signature

_____   _____, a Florida Corporation

_____   By: _____

value from the employer. At the time a job is offered, it may be tendered on the condition that the employee will not compete after he leaves the job. This kind of an arrangement is usually held valid, since the job was given with the understanding that this would be expected of the worker.

If the employee is already on the job when the employer demands that he sign a noncompete agreement, however, the courts will usually say that the employee was not given anything for his promise. He already had his job, and he had no reasonable opportunity to refuse to sign the agreement without jeopardizing his job. Therefore, goes the logic of the courts, the agreement is not enforceable against the worker. In order for an agreement to be legally recognized as a contract, something of value must be given or must be promised by each side to the agreement. As a matter of public policy, the courts are hesitant to restrict a man's right to earn a living unless it is clear that he wants to give it up in exchange for a definite benefit.

Generally, too, noncompete agreements are not held valid by the courts if they are too broad in application. A company that does business in only one locality and obtains a promise from an employee to refrain from competition even in a distant part of the state will usually not be upheld in the courts. A noncompete agreement of this type with a nationwide company would probbly be enforced, however. It is therefore desirable for the noncompete agreement to define the territorial area in which it is to apply. If the ban on the employee is wider than is necessary to protect the company, it will be regarded as invalid by the courts.

section two

PERSONNEL PRACTICES
FOR PREVENTION AND CONTROL

14

Company Rules and Records

THROUGHOUT the preceding chapters detailing instances of employee misconduct, the duty of management to state and make known rules and regulations regarding employee conduct was frequently pointed out. In many of the examples given of arbitration decisions that went against management, the principal reason cited by the arbitrator was that the company had not clearly stated and adequately circulated a ruling on the matter involved. Accurate records of evidence of employee performance and behavior also can help to prove management's case.

The responsibility for circulating employee rules and supervising compliance with them usually rests with the personnel department. It is here that matters of pay, benefits, absenteeism, and control of employees are centered. The department is also held responsible for maintaining records of employee behavior and performance and for the hiring and firing of all company personnel.

Company rules and records are the tools the personnel department uses in preventing or controlling the various types of employee misconduct. Rules provide guidelines for employee behavior, and records assure fair and equitable treatment of all employees.

If management intends for employees to abide by specific company rules, it is obvious that these rules must be made known to the employees. Statutes and administrative regulations in some states require that employee rules be posted on bulletin boards located in prominent places throughout the business or industrial establishment. This may be the most forceful and effective way of bringing rules to the attention of workers. Some companies also publish employee handbooks which explain rules, as well as giving valuable information on rights and benefits.

Verbal briefing may be used to inform rank-and-file workers, either individually or in groups. The claim can always be made that verbal instructions were not heard or understood, however. Arbitrators and the courts are inclined to hold with employees unless there is every reason to believe that they should have known the company standards.

Initial Employment Briefing

Some firms follow the practice of briefing each new worker individually as to the company rules at the time he or she begins employment. Individual attention of this kind promotes the new employee's identification with the company and helps to emphasize the importance of company rules.

Because new personnel may be bewildered when confronted with a mass of forms, routines, and regulations, some firms defer briefing until a few days after they have assumed their duties. The argument is that company rules will mean more to new employees who have had a few days to assimilate company procedures and understand how individual regulations fit into the work routine.

A major New York wholesale company with branches throughout the United States which was having difficulty in bringing company rules to the attention of newly hired persons set out all of the company rules on two sides of a single sheet of paper. After the new individual had been on the job for approximately a week, he or she was requested to review each rule with the personnel representative and to sign the sheet as an indication that each company requirement was understood.

When individual rules are not clear to the new worker, the personnel representative goes into detail to explain the workings of the rule and why it is needed. At the conclusion of this interview session, the employee is again requested to sign the sheet, certifying that he is aware of the company regulations and understands his duties and responsibilities.

This signed sheet is then retained in the employee's permanent personnel file. If the worker thereafter is involved in misconduct, it is difficult for him to plead ignorance of the rules.

Deliberately Ignoring Rules

Some employees seem to want to stay at odds with management, deliberately violating rules such as those against smoking in prohibited areas or horseplay on the job. There is no guarantee as to how a labor arbitrator will decide in such cases. Arbitrators are not necessarily bound by precedent, and each situation must be evaluated on its individual merits.

Management can build a strong case for discharge or discipline when no-smoking rules are violated, for example, by following these steps:

1. Make certain that the no-smoking requirements are spelled out to new employees at the time they are hired.
2. Be sure the rules are stated clearly in the company manual or personnel booklet.
3. Follow a procedure of posting the rules on the bulletin board or repeating them at company meetings.

4. Post clearly legible signs in prominent locations in areas where smoking is not permitted.

To prevent company loss from employee horseplay or pranksterism, management must have definite rules prohibiting this type of activity. Suspension or discharge, as determined by the extent and frequency of this misconduct, should be imposed as the penalty.

Horseplay always results in waste of productive time. It usually distracts far more employees than those who are actually involved. In some instances, a worker may cause serious physical harm to another, and the company may be held responsible for the resulting injury.

Falsification of Records

Falsification of company records can take many forms. Practically all examples of this kind of activity involve alterations designed to increase employee paychecks or to confer benefits that were not earned. If there is no control over access to office records, for example, employees may falsify the number of days of vacation leave taken or the number of days of sick leave available so additional vacation time or sick leave can be claimed.

One of the most common types of falsification occurs when one employee punches the time card of another so he can arrive late or depart early. Management can spot check attendance in a few minutes' time by taking employee attendance cards from the time rack at random and physically verifying the presence of the employee whose name is on each card. This technique should be applied on a nonscheduled basis. It may also occasionally be advisable to compare the hours represented by clock entries on the time card with the weekly list of hours worked by the individual. If discrepancies are noted, an investigation should be immediately conducted to determine whether this is a regular happening.

Management has encountered considerable opposition in discharging employees who have falsified work records, particularly in companies where workers are represented by labor unions. When a union member is caught in this type of activity, union representatives may maintain that he merely made a regrettable clerical mistake, without any intention to falsify his work record. In many instances of this kind there is no way of proving if the actual motive of the employee was to defraud the company.

Other records that are frequently falsified involve incentive quotas. If the output level of an employee determines the amount of his pay, it is not unusual for falsification to take place. In some instances this may involve connivance between the employee and a supervisor in counting the volume of piecework.

A typical example is in the production area of an industrial laundry or linen plant where a worker is paid a bonus or incentive on the basis of the number of sheets run through an ironer or some similar production process. The majority of supervisors in such an installation will be found to be completely reliable. However, due in part to the low pay scale in the industry, it may be noted that the supervisor will go along with employee falsification. In a situation of this kind, management may be able to verify whether fraud has occurred by adding the total production figures for all employees and comparing the figures given with the total of all employee incentive quotas and regular production figures.

Expense Account Padding

Some firms expect sales employees to pad expense accounts, while others will make a searching examination of every claim on an expense account. In a recent case in a western state, a salesman incurred the wrath of the company president when he organized his co-workers into a union. Shortly thereafter, the salesman was called into the president's office and discharged for padding his expense account.

The salesman admitted that he had followed a practice of making liberal entries on his expense account, in accordance with the practices that were sanctioned by the company for all sales personnel. He maintained that his expense account entries were in accordance with the standards approved by the company for himself and other sales personnel in the past and claimed that he had been discharged because of his union activities. After a hearing before the National Labor Relations Board, the president of the corporation told news representatives that the salesman had been discharged for cheating on his expense account. The salesman countered by filing a libel and slander suit against the company.

When this matter came to trial, the court pointed out that a company had a right to discharge an individual who was caught falsifying an expense account. The court also noted, however, that in a case like this where company salesmen were allowed to include certain charges on a regular basis, the company had no right to complain when salesmen continued this practice. Since these inflated amounts on expense accounts had been condoned by the company in the past, the court indicated that such claims for reimbursement could not be regarded as dishonest in this instance. The court held that a finding of slander would be proper since the company had blackened the salesman's name for a practice it had previously condoned.[1]

Payroll Padding

An illegal act that can cause considerable company loss is payroll padding, or the placing of fictitious names on the company payroll. A New York shipping firm discovered that paychecks printed in the names of nonexistent employees were subsequently cashed by the supervisor who was responsible for adding these

[1] *Washer* v. *Bank of America National Trust & Savings Assn.*, 136 p 2d 297.

"ghosts" to the payroll. The loss totaled more than a quarter of a million dollars.

After this experience, the company comptroller no longer allowed payroll lists to be complied without verification. Each section chief prepared the payroll for his own department, but in addition an employee of the comptroller was assigned to verify the existence of each person on the payroll list on a regular basis. As an additional safeguard, from time to time the comptroller had each paycheck distributed to the employee who had earned it. A dishonest section chief would not dare step forward to claim a check that had been printed for a fictitious person.

The comptroller also introduced another control to make certain that this kind of fraud did not arise a second time. When a new employee was hired, his name was placed on a list of workers in the section to which he was assigned. Similarly, his name was deleted if he was terminated. The list that was compiled in this manner was placed in the computer records. When payroll checks were printed by the computer, a comparison was made between the checks and the master employee list. If other names appeared on payroll checks, or if the totals did not correspond, the computer was programmed to print out a warning for the comptroller.

Overpayment of Employees

In a Chicago case, a maintenance man was underpaid on one occasion. The worker immediately took this matter to the payroll office, and the shortage was corrected. In a number of instances thereafter, the employee was consistently overpaid. When the company matched payroll information with time cards, it was apparent that the accounting clerk compiling the records had been systematically recording more overtime than the employee had worked.

When management showed the records to the accounting clerk,

he immediately submitted his resignation but declined to be interviewed about record falsification. The maintenance employee who had directly benefited by this scheme refused to resign or admit to any wrongdoing. He was discharged and later filed a grievance, claiming that he was being blamed for errors committed by the accounting clerk.

When the matter came to arbitration, the hearing officer found that the maintenance man had not falsified any records himself. He did find, however, that the employee's pay records had been deliberately altered for five consecutive compensation periods. The worker made no effort to explain these alterations, and he failed to report the over-payments.

The union representative got the company accountant to admit that about 90 percent of the firm's workers had been incorrectly paid at some time or other. The accountant also admitted that only a handful of employees had ever come to a company representative when they believed that they had been overpaid.

The arbitrator ruled in favor of the firm noting however, that the overpayments in this case were so large and so continuous that a reasonable employee in this position should have known that he was receiving more than he was due. If the errors had been slight and had not involved a deliberate falsification of records, the arbitrator indicated that he would have held otherwise.[2] The arbitrator sustained the company's decision, even though it was doubtful that there was enough evidence to justify a criminal prosecution.

Management Control of Records

When a dismissal made on the basis of record falsification comes to trial or arbitration the company must be able to show

[2] *Duval Corporation, Mineral Park Property* and *United Steelworkers of America, Local 6850,* 71–1 ARB 8060.

that records were properly maintained. If the union representative is able to demonstrate that mistakes are frequently made and that supervisory controls are haphazard, there is a likelihood that an arbitrator may reinstate an employee who has been dismissed because of this charge.[3] Management therefore has a responsibility to make certain that complacency about record keeping will not erode the employer's right to discipline a dishonest worker.

There are a number of basic steps employers can take to protect company records. First a rule pointing out that all data, records, and compiled information used on the job are company property should be posted prominently on the company bulletin board and set forth in the employee manual. If individuals are allowed to take records or data files from the office, a receipt acknowledging company ownership should be obtained.

If the information is confidential, it should be stamped as such with a rubber stamp or marked in some manner to indicate that it should not be allowed in the possession of unauthorized persons.

Termination interviews for workers should include procedures for recovering all company property and records. It should be pointed out that employees are not allowed to take anything from the premises except items that are clearly personal property and have not been used in any way in connection with job assignments. This is discussed further in Chapter 19.

---

[3] In re *Duval Sulpher and Potash Company* (Carlsbad, N.M.) and *International Union of Mine Mill, and Smelter Workers, Carlsbad Potash Workers Local 415* (Ind.) Case No. 54A–240, November 7, 1953, 21 LA 560.

15

Control of Absenteeism

ABSENTEEISM may be one of the most costly employee activities to plague organizational efficiency. Directly or indirectly, it can lead to poor customer relations, cancellation of longstanding accounts, scheduling tie-ups, and countless other forms of loss. As a result of this kind of employee misconduct, production is crippled and conscientious employees who do report for work are saddled with extra duties that may be unfamiliar.

One authority indicates that "absenteeism is costing industry upwards of $10 billion per year, and only half of it is due to sickness."[1] No company objects to valid absenteeism, but it is reasonable to doubt the loyalty of the healthy employee who remains away from the job.

Good personnel record keeping is essential to the control of absenteeism. Not only must the firm be able to determine each employee's attendance record, but written notices of violations are often necessary if dismissal actions for absenteeism are to be

---

[1] Raymond Dreyfack, *How to Control Absenteeism* (Chicago, Dartnell Corp., 1972), p. 3.

upheld in the courts or by arbitrators. The right to discharge for excessive absenteeism, especially when there is an established policy regarding this problem, has usually been upheld, but there are cases in which the firing of chronically absent employees was reversed in arbitration because no warnings or suspensions had been given for earlier similar infractions. Such notices, coupled with good record keeping, almost assures that all cases of abuse of the absence privilege will be disciplined fairly, regardless of the offender's seniority.

In one recent case, a worker with 15 years of service was fired for unexcused absence. He had always performed well on the job, but after a time he started to lay off from work without prior permission or for any legitimate reason. Frequently, the firm was not advised about his being gone until he returned to duty the following day.

Management took the attitude that the absence of a single employee could adversely affect production schedules, and each individual therefore has a responsibility to make every reasonable effort to be at work. This employee had been warned on three earlier occasions and had been suspended on the last of these absences. When he was later discharged, he had not only been absent without approval but had lied to the supervisor about the reason for his being gone. Although the union opposition in this case was strong, the arbitrator upheld the action of management.

Absenteeism is also used as a reason for denying a promotion to an employee, although labor contracts may make it difficult for management to utilize this reason for preferring an employee with less seniority in a specific instance. If the promotion clause in the union contract is broadly drawn, arbitrators may be inclined to overlook the fact that the preferred employee has had far less absenteeism than another and therefore they will refuse to consider this as a fair reason for ignoring seniority.

The promotion clause of one union agreement read "promotion

to higher pay jobs or better jobs with equal pay shall be determined as follows: physical fitness and ability being equal, plant seniority shall prevail." The company maintained that an employee with a great deal of seniority who had a record of absences and late arrivals was not entitled to consideration for a position involving more responsibility. The union argued against this, but the arbitrator held that to ignore the poor attendance record of the senior employee would be to condone inattention to job responsibility. The arbitrator also pointed out that although the more tenured employee had not been warned about his absenteeism or suspended, the employer could use his poor record as a basis for making an evaluation of the employees contending for the position.

Unjustified versus Excessive Absence

Most of this chapter deals with *unjustified* or unexcused absenteeism. This involves instances where an employee may quit work early without permission, call in ill when he or she actually is not, fail to notify a supervisor of being out, or be discovered holding down a second job while receiving sick pay from a first job.

There are also many cases of *excessive* absence. These may involve the worker with a lingering illness or one who stays out too late at night, which may result in missing a few days each month. In some instances, employees' excessive absences could be due to a disability resulting from failure to have needed surgery performed. Often in this situation, less time will be spent away from the job during a month-long postoperative recuperation period than in skipping a few days each month for many years. In such cases of justified yet excessive absenteeism, counseling with direct supervisors and members of the personnel and medical departments may be helpful.

Another type of worker who is excessively absent is the one with a known or disguised alcohol or drug abuse problem. These problems are detailed in Chapters 2 and 3.

The Friday to Monday Weekend

Some firms that have paydays on Thursdays and Fridays experience production difficulties due to poor absence control. Often this happens because following the receipt of their pay envelope on Friday, many employees embark on a weekend-long binge of alcohol and drugs. Some workers just show up long enough on Friday to be paid, and Monday is often devoted to taking care of hangovers. The problem is so widespread that some experts feel it is best not to purchase a car that was made on a Monday or a Friday. On these two days, many unskilled workers have to be given more technical jobs hastily on a temporary basis, to cover the duties of workers who are missing and keep the production line flowing. Such a substitute worker, while having the best of intentions, could spend the day installing a part incorrectly, and the incorrect fitting of this part that could be difficult for quality control inspectors to detect.

Suggestions for coping with this problem include biweekly or monthly rather than weekly paydays and improving multiple-duty training. Such steps, however, do not correct the cause of the problem.

Notification

Many organizations require employees who are going to be away from the job to contact their supervisors beforehand. It is usually stipulated that notification must be from the worker himself or his immediate family and must be given directly to the immediate supervisor, not to a co-worker who is entrusted with relaying the message. Suspensions of absent workers have been sustained in arbitration for this action because of the resulting confusion of such a practice or in cases where the co-worker forgot to deliver the message.

A worker who informs the boss that he will be out the next day, who is told not to do this, and then without reason fails to show up for work has given the mandatory notification but has disobeyed other rules of the organization. In one case of this nature the worker was fired but, because an arbitrator felt that he had showed some prudence in giving notification (although the request was turned down), he was reinstated in his job without pay for the time lost. Such a situation leaves the supervisor open to some criticism for not checking into the reason for the absence.

Checking the Excuse

The procedure of checking reasons for absence by making verification calls to the employee's home can be helpful in curbing absenteeism. The worker then knows that the supervisor is aware of the absence, which might not otherwise be the case in a large department. If the phone rings and there is no answer, about the only way the employee can explain this is to prove that he or she was at a pharmacy obtaining medicine or at the doctor's office.

Many governmental agencies and businesses require that a doctor's written excuse be brought to the supervisor after three days of absence. The reason for setting this time limit is that three days is the usual time necessary to find another job. If there is no doctor's excuse after three days and the employee is still absent, management may declare the position vacant.

A rule requiring that employees who wish to leave work early or to take time off for legitimate reasons must speak directly to their immediate supervisors provides an obvious opportunity to probe the reason for the missed time. Merely allowing an employee to call in to any other worker whenever he or she is going to be off is not enough. A casual "Tell the boss I won't be in this morning" can be forgotten by the co-worker. Experience has shown that the easier it is to be absent, the more frequent absences will become.

The supervisor checking the excuses of ill employees should ask for details about the sickness or injury. This must be done tactfully but without undue sympathy, to discourage absence when malingering is a possibility. A spot check of the personnel records, which should specify the type of illness or injuries that have been responsible for any previous need to be off work, can make it possible for the supervisor to state his recollection of similar occurrences to the worker. This shows concern for the employee and at the same time lets him know that records are being kept. Where appropriate, the supervisor can suggest a medical checkup for a recurring problem.

Employees who are found to have given a false reason for absence are usually dismissed. It can be expected that dismissal for this reason will be sustained in labor arbitration decisions, provided, of course, that the incident is not the first offense and proper warnings have been given for earlier violations.

Obviously sick individuals such as those with bad coughs should be encouraged to take sick leave. It may be necessary for management to send such employees home so they do not spread communicable diseases through the entire work force. A worker who is ill and tries to remain on the job also will not produce up to standards and may slow down other workers.

Rules prohibiting workers from taking second jobs or moonlighting are designed to prevent conflict of interest or to discourage the disclosure of trade secrets. Even if these two acts of disloyalty are not involved and the firm's rules avoid mentioning outside employment, the employer may resent a worker holding down a second job or running a small "cottage industry" at home. An employee who works more than one job will not give full measure to his primary employer and may become so tired that time off is necessary.

One employee, on the orders of his doctor, was off work and receiving sick pay because of a diagnosed neurotic condition. Management became aware that the individual was still operating a small firm and fired him. When the case was arbitrated, the findings were in the worker's favor because while he was under extreme stress in his first job, the pressure was considerably less at his own business. The second job was medically regarded as beneficial therapy.[2]

Properly handled, management could have questioned this employee about how he was passing his time away from the firm and possibly assigned him to less tension-causing duties until he was fully recovered. Thus some benefit could have been received by the company, and needed therapy could have been gained by the worker.

Extended Coffee Breaks: On-the-Job Vacations

Some people feel that the coffee break is one of the greatest innovations since sliced bread. But it can be costly. A worker who is paid $5 per hour and extends his coffee break by 10 minutes each day will waste over 41 hours per year, at an annual cost of over $200. This is for only *one* worker, and there could be many more in the same situation. The company receives nothing in return for the individual's yearly extra free week of on-the-job vacation.

Abuses of this nature have led management in some cases to consider abandoning the coffee break. Even if there is no union

[2] In re *United States Steel Corporation, Tennessee Coal & Iron Division, Fairfield Steel Workers and United Steelworkers of America, Local 1013,* Case No. T–381, June 29, 1956, 26 LA 712.

contract which mandates rest periods, second thoughts are in order. Tightening up discipline on abuses of the rest period is the most realistic way to cope with this problem.

One employer considered having coffee delivered to his people so that they would supposedly not be inconvenienced by having to leave their work stations. This would not have been much of a favor. The purpose of the coffee break (or, more appropriately, the rest period) is to provide a temporary intermission of labor away from the work environment. It is designed to alleviate pressures that naturally build up on the job and to give employees a reasonable amount of time to get a second wind. Coffee breaks are as much a benefit to management as to the worker because it has been shown that production which would ordinarily fall off without the respite tends to pick up after the break.

Leaving Work Early

Intention is a major factor in determining corrective action when faced with an individual who quits work early or otherwise walks off the job. If the worker intended to quit altogether, dismissal is proper.

Discharges have been questioned in separate cases in which a worker left early without permission and another employee unexpectedly walked off the job for the remainder of the day to control his temper after an argument with a supervisor. Under arbitration, lighter punishment was given in both cases because there was nothing to show that the workers had meant to sever employment with their firms. Neither had requested a final paycheck, and they had not turned in the equipment and tools issued to them. The first individual was given a short suspension, while the second was reinstated with loss of back pay.

A different employer came out on top in a similar situation, but just barely. When a worker told his supervisor he was leaving early to take care of personal business, the foreman refused to give permission. The worker left anyway and, upon returning later, was not penalized. The second time this happened, however, the foreman had the employee fired.

In finding for the company in this case, the arbitrator noted that such action was reasonable on the foreman's part, but he should have indicated more strongly that the first walk-off was a violation that could jeopardize the worker's job if it were repeated. It is always good practice to tell rule-breakers straightforwardly where continued offenses will lead them.

Midweek holidays often are troublesome in the matter of early quitters. Arbitration decisions have been fairly consistent in upholding disciplinary steps such as canceling holiday pay when, without prior approval, an employee tries to extend a weekend through a holiday, thereby upsetting production schedules. Union contracts often read that a person must work both the day before and the day after a holiday to receive holiday pay. While a manager can sympathize with a worker's desire to avoid heavy holiday traffic by getting a head start on a short vacation trip, the manager's responsibility for maintaining his department's production quota is of overriding importance.

The Exhausted Worker

It is usually true that an employee's free time is his own and his pursuits in private are his own business. But when his off-time activities negatively affect his performance, then it becomes a matter for the employer's concern. It is only reasonable to expect each worker to get adequate rest so that his output will not be impaired due to lack of mental alertness and physical stamina. If the employee is truly sick, management does not expect or intend that he should work.

In one case of this kind, a worker reported to his union steward that he doubted he would be able to work through the shift, since he had slept for only about an hour the night before. The worker explained that he had been celebrating with two of his nephews who had just returned to the United States from overseas military service and that he had consumed "two beers" with them. After remaining on the job for a short time, the worker informed his foreman that he was very tired and asked to be relieved. The foreman agreed but asked the employee to continue on the job for a short time. During this period, the worker ruined a piece of machine work and was told to go home. He was suspended for five days.

This suspension was appealed to arbitration by the union. The facts brought out indicated that the employee had been doing some drinking but was definitely not under the influence of liquor. He had been sent home because he was so exhausted he was not able to perform his job properly or reasonably. The arbitrator ruled that under circumstances of this kind the employer could impose discipline, and the five-day suspension was suitable.

Modern living conditions contribute to worker exhaustion. Sprawling suburban communities tend to spread away from business and industrial centers, so employees must spend more time on crowded freeways in getting to and from jobs. Staggered work shifts and the adoption of a four-day work week could help to eliminate part of this congestion. Some firms have attempted to reduce fatigue and automobile pollution by offering free parking to employees who travel in car pools. While this does not cut down the time spent on the road, it does alleviate some of the driver strain.

To some extent this problem can be avoided when new applicants are interviewed in the hiring process. Caution should be exercised, however, not to deny employment on the basis of where the applicant resides. It can be pointed out to an applicant that necessary travel time can add considerably to the daily commitment, and therefore it may be advisable to move closer to work if possible. Personnel representatives in some firms help transferees find suitable homes near the company's local branch.

While inner-city living may be depressing due to blight, pollution, and high rent, some applicants might be advised that it could be preferable for them to live downtown if that is the location of the business. Such advice may be particularly helpful to individuals who are seeking a first job or are new to a metropolitan area. Management thus advises the new worker that he or she is expected to arrive on time in the morning. This advice also can point out that living close to work can mean more leisure time, so on-the-job production does not suffer.

Methods of Prevention and Control

Management can reduce the high toll taken by absenteeism through a variety of procedures. One way of coping with absenteeism that is due to authentic sickness is to offer employees free annual innoculations against influenza. These are usually obtainable during work hours, and employees are not docked for taking time off to get them. This program has had considerable success and is being adopted by the private sector through arrangements with company doctors or paid for by the firm at outside clinics.

Meeting the demands of safety requirements can reduce time lost due to accidental injuries. Often safety programs are morale boosters because they indicate management's concern for the well-being of workers.

A primary means of preventing and controlling absenteeism is good personnel record keeping. Accurate records are essential to reward those with good attendance histories and to detect and later discipline the offenders if necessary. Such records are required to back up suspensions and dismissals if there is a grievance or if cases are arbitrated.

It is equally important to post clearly understood rules which show the employee what the limits are. In many cases management has tried to assure employees that such rules are not witch hunts by allowing a 5- to 15-minute leeway on tardiness, provided the missed time is made up. This is necessary in large metropolitan areas where traffic and parking are real problems, even to conscientious persons who allow themselves ample time to get to work.

Confidential interviews by supervisors and managers with employees who are habitually tardy, overextend rest periods, or are absent too frequently can also be effective. In this way management shows it is aware of the worker's negligence and explores the positive steps that can be taken for correction. Such interviews demonstrate the need for prompt, continuous attendance and negate the attitude of "they'll never miss me." The reality of discharge for such seemingly small offenses can be brought home to the workers, who may not realize how serious the practices are.

Incentives for loyal workers have also cut down absenteeism and tardiness. Hartford Insurance Company gives one paid day off for 13 weeks of continuous work. Other employers have a policy of counseling tenured workers when they have not abused the privilege of sick leave but have had to use all of their accrued sick pay. With a written explanation from medical authorities detailing a need for additional sick time, the worker is only allowed to accrue half of his normal vacation time per month, and the other half goes to make up the deficient sick leave. Such a plan, or a temporary pay reduction, is only recommended for workers with long-time service who are using up sick leave at an alarming rate but who should be kept in the organization.

Many businesses and governmental agencies allow up to half of a person's sick leave time to be used for family illnesses. Few parents, for example, could perform adequately on the job if they have a child home or in the hospital with a serious sickness or injury. Such a policy of sick pay when an immediate family member—and not the worker—is incapacitated tends to create loyalty to the employer.

Earlier retirement is permitted by some organizations through a two-for-one conversion of unused sick-leave days for vacation time which is compensated for at the full pay rate. Some firms with a high number of female employees who need time for gift shopping give workers an extra day off before the Christmas holidays if they have stayed under a certain limit of absences.

Controlling Absenteeism through Employee Attitudes

Management can also help solve the problem by exploring the causes of unexplained or unexcused absences. For the man who is bright and good at his job, chronic absence may be a symptom of boredom with his present assignment. This individual could perhaps handle more responsibility. Others who have risen to well-paying positions early in their careers may have remained in these jobs too long. They find that their positions are dull but fairly secure, and they lack the courage to seek a more demanding job elsewhere. To them also, absence is a good way to break the monotony. If such employees are given more duties and better pay on a trial basis, their attendance should improve.

Employees either help or harm firms through their efforts and their attitudes. The valuable employee is on hand when needed, and reliably turns out the work management depends on him to produce. To some extent, attitudes of value to the company can be nurtured by letting employees know what reliability is appreciated. But if management can cultivate real pride in achievement among employees, a great deal more can be accomplished. If all employees are encouraged to feel that their own jobs are important to the success of the firm, absenteeism will be diminished.

16

Control of Persons on the Business Premises

If a business office or industrial installation is on private property, the owners or managers have the right to set up whatever security controls they believe are necessary. If stringent controls are not handled in a diplomatic manner, however, employees may be offended.

Control of Employees Entering or Leaving

A Philadelphia firm had a company rule instructing plant guards to inspect all briefcases and packages taken out by workers. This requirement was to be applied to everyone. In practice, the uniformed guards did not inspect briefcases carried by union representatives, however. This was partly due to respect for the union and partly because the company did not want to be accused of harassing union officials.

Near the end of a shift, a foreman observed a union steward concealing a valuable tool behind a vending machine. Concluding that the steward intended to steal the tool, the foreman advised

149

the guard at the exit gate. When the steward started to leave the plant shortly thereafter, the guard asked to be allowed to inspect his briefcase.

The steward adamantly refused to open the case, shouting, "It contains union business, and that's confidential!" The guard called the corporate security officer and the plant superintendent, who explained to the steward that no one was exempt from the examination requirement and that the rule was well known to the union and to everyone else on the premises. The steward persisted in his refusal and was discharged on the spot.

The following day he returned with other union officials, claiming that he was merely trying to protect the confidential nature of the union records he was carrying. Other labor officials argued that a request to examine a briefcase under these circumstances was an invasion of the steward's privacy, as well as that of the union itself.

Management explained that the facts indicated the steward may have committed a crime and that the guard was trying to prove or disprove this issue, not to look into confidential papers. It was pointed out that allowing a guard to take a quick glance at the contents of a briefcase was different from permitting him to review confidential material or reports. Management assured the union that such activity on the part of the guards would not be tolerated.

In reviewing company procedures in this case, it was pointed out that uniformed guards were under orders to make a cursory check of the outside of all briefcases. If suspicion of the contents developed, the guards were under instructions to request that the case be opened. Refusal under these circumstances was to be treated as an admission of guilt, and the penalty for theft at this firm had always been immediate discharge. This explanation prompted the union to withdraw support from the complaining steward, and his request for reinstatement was not pressed. The labor officials were convinced that the search in question was directed at the control of theft and not at an inspection of union records.

The important conclusions to be drawn from situations of this kind are that security procedures should be uniformly applied, and the search should be limited to the control of loss.

Once conditions for entry and departure from the firm's property are set up, they must be applied impartially. Care should be taken that a particular class of worker, ethnic group, or any specialized type of person is not singled out in making searches, and the inspection must be directed toward the control of company property or merchandise or the protection of employees, rather than an examination of confidential papers.

Searchers on Government Property

Some members of the public have contended that a private business may have the right to search persons coming and going on the premises but that the federal government has no such right. This is based on the idea that federal property belongs to everyone, and no one should be restricted.

In a case on this point, the U.S. General Services Administration issued instructions as follows: "During hours when the building is open, persons entering the building with briefcases, packages, etc. will be required to show ID cards or have their packages inspected." Shortly after this system was started in Nashville, Tennessee, a lawyer declined to allow such an inspection. Arguing that his papers were confidential, he maintained that only his client had the right to examine them.

General Services Administration officials then gave the attorney three choices:

1. He could permit an inspection.

2. He could check his briefcase with the guard and go on about his business in the building.
3. He could carry the briefcase as long as he would agree to be accompanied by a guard.

The attorney declined to submit to any of these controls, claiming that his rights had been violated. When the matter came to trial, the U.S. district judge stated emphatically that the United States was not helpless in protecting its property once it had been opened for the public use.

In holding for reasonable government inspection, the judge continued:

The United States can control entrance to its property by conditioning the entrant's right of entry on his submitting his packages and briefcase to a visual inspection.

Where the protection of government property and personnel from destruction is balanced against any invasion of personal dignity, privacy and constitutional rights, the government's interest in conducting the cursory inspection outweighs the personal inconvenience suffered by the individual.

In commenting on this case, the federal judge also noted that private businesses have the definite right to deny or restrict entry or to utilize whatever restrictions they consider necessary as a condition for allowing access.[1]

Package Passes

A control procedure designed to prevent unauthorized removal of materials from the premises involves the issuance of passes for all packages taken off company property. A typical package pass is shown in Figure 4. This pass is numerically controlled, and a copy is retained in a supervisor's book for comparison.

When a firm in Manhattan experienced repeated losses of company typewriters, a system was installed requiring every person

---

[1] *Barrett* v. *Kunzig,* 331 F. Supp. 266.

FIGURE 4
Typical Package Pass

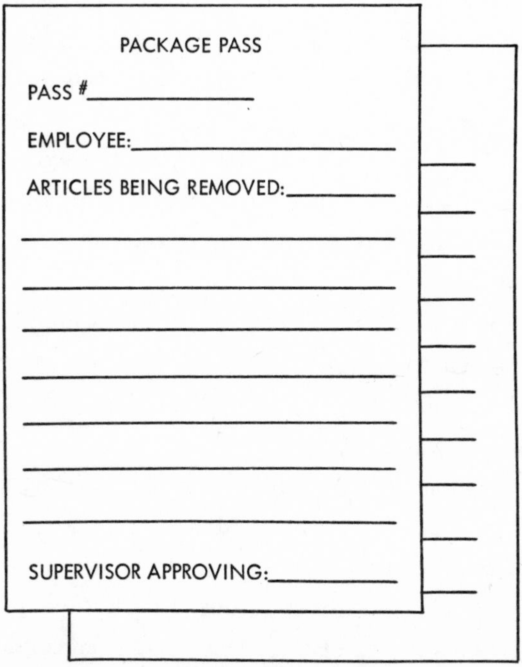

PACKAGE PASS

PASS #_____

EMPLOYEE:_____

ARTICLES BEING REMOVED:_____

_____

_____

_____

_____

_____

_____

_____

SUPERVISOR APPROVING:_____

A Sample Package Pass, Numerically Controlled,
with a Copy Retained in the Supervisor's Book for
Comparison.

removing a package from the building to obtain a package pass,
signed by a department head. Elevator operators in this company-
owned building were already regulating the entry of everyone
coming into the building on week-ends or after hours, and they
were instructed to collect package passes and to make a brief
visual inspection of any article being taken from the building.
As a verification of this system, package passes are collected on
a daily basis, and the signatures on the passes are inspected for
authenticity. Use of this system brought an end to the typewriter
losses. Employees voiced no objection once the system was explained to them.

Sporadic Searches of Employees

A company rule used in a Detroit, Michigan, automobile assembly plant stipulated that "An employee taking out a parcel shall obtain a pass from his foreman. It must be given to the guard—and the parcel submitted for inspection."

Uniformed guards at this plant occasionally used a spot check technique. Sometimes they went for months without challenging anyone. When a search was finally made, the parcels selected were taken at random.

One employee was requested to submit to a search but declined and was allowed to depart. A month later the same man was again asked to submit to a search. When he refused a second time, the worker was discharged.

The labor union at this plant demanded reinstatement of the employee, but the firm declined. Management argued that spot checks serve to discourage pilferage and that every employer has the right to conduct such inspections. In addition, the company representatives maintained that searches had been conducted many times previously, so that this technique had become an accepted practice.

The arbitrator who ruled on this matter ordered the reinstatement of the worker. He pointed out that the company handbook made no mention of the fact that employees might be subjected to searches and seemed to emphasize that spot checks in the past had been very infrequent and that no real pattern had been established.

The arbitrator indicated that he would have upheld the company's right to search if the application form signed by job seekers had contained an agreement that they would allow themselves to be searched and if the purpose of such a program was fully explained to workers.

From these cases it seems evident that a company does not have an actual legal right to search workers. What management does have is a right to impose conditions on employees or anyone else coming onto the property such that they either agree to a search as a condition for gaining admittance to the premises or they are not allowed to enter.

Therefore, the firm should set the stage for the search privilege. The employment application should contain an agreement signed by the worker, consenting to reasonable searches as a condition for employment. In addition, this requirement should be brought to the attention of all personnel by including it in printed sets of security rules and in the company handbook and by posting an appropriate notice on departmental bulletin boards. Verbal briefing given at the time of hiring may also be used as proof that the worker was placed on notice.

Searches should be made with enough frequency that a pattern of prior searches can be established. It is also necessary to apply these searches impartially, requiring employees of all ranks to participate.

Employee Lockers

Some firms have experienced serious disputes by making indiscriminate searches of employee locker. Even though lockers are located on company property and are paid for with company funds, some workers come to regard these areas as their personal property.

Experience shows that pilfered items are frequently stored in employee lockers. This is another area where management should consider searches only with appropriate caution, however. Workers may have a legitimate complaint if locks are broken during an inspection. It is therefore suggested that a written rule be in effect requiring permission to search as a condition for allowing employee occupancy of the lockers. It is also suggested that the

use of company-owned locks only should be required, with duplicate keys to be retained by management. If the search technique
is used, it should be directed toward all lockers without bias.

Employees Who Work Unsupervised—
Janitorial, Temporary, and Maintenance Employees

Every business must place some reliance on the personal integrity of the individuals who work for it. But while it is desirable
for trust to be placed in employees, management has the responsibility of maintaining controls to protect the business from misconduct or carelessness by all its personnel. This includes not only
full-time and temporary employees but those who work unsupervised during off hours.

A firm that closely restricts access after closing hours and on
the weekend and limits the possession of door keys to a few members of management at the same time may provide open doors
to maintenance workers or employees of an outside janitorial
firm. Often these are individuals who are never known to management. In effect, this assumes that proven employees are likely to
commit thefts or other crimes against the company but there is
little likelihood that unknown maintenance or janitorial employees will do so. Such an attitude is not realistic.

This is not to say that all maintenance or janitorial workers
are dishonest. Many of these individuals remain with one company
for years and prove to be models of honesty and dependability.
But the employee of a contract janitorial service is an outsider
with a reason to be inside, a man or woman who may not have
the same basic loyalties that are to be expected in a regular
worker. What this means is that a company may buy a service,
but management does not thereby do away with the responsibility
to manage.

Frequently, these outside individuals will turn out to be marginally employable in the labor market due to unusual background problems or arrest records. In some instances they may be limited only ecause of insufficient training, lack of polish, or unfamiliarity with the social graces. But they may also be unable to hold more steady jobs because of low moral standards.

It is worth noting that financial need is sometimes an inducement to theft or other crime. Janitorial workers may face more temptation to become involved in theft because they receive comparatively low pay and work undesirable shifts. It is on these night shifts that they may have more opportunity for wrongdoing without being observed.

Because of the nature of the job, janitorial employees can become completely familiar with the buildings in which they work. They know the means of ingress and usually become quite familiar with the use of alarm systems and locks. They may also gain intimate knowledge of any patrol or guard service that is used and may use this knowledge either to commit a theft or to set up a burglary or other crime for outside criminals.

Curtailing Janitorial Access

One way to control the possibility of misconduct by janitorial and maintenance workers is to curtail their access to company property. In some cases it may be practical for cleaning services to be performed during regular business hours. If operational areas are crowded with daytime workers, however, the janitor may not be able to perform his tasks without interfering with routine functions. Another disadvantage is that a lawsuit may result if someone slips on a newly scrubbed floor or is struck by a waxing machine.

A janitor who goes about his duties during regular business hours may become so familiar that no one will question his coming and going in warehouse or stockroom areas. If he receives little supervision, he may not attract attention when removing merchandise from the building.

Some firms assign a management employee to supervise cleaning done after hours. Others rekey building locks so that the cleaning employee has access to one area only. This is no proof against loss, however.

One janitorial employee was furnished a key that allowed access to a firm's office only. Money and stamps, as well as vital records, were secured in the office safe, and there was nothing in the area that seemed attractive to a thief. The warehouse immediately behind the office, however, was filled with small appliances and electrical goods. In exploring the building, the janitor found that there was a false ceiling over the office area. By pushing upward on some of the acoustical ceiling panels, he discovered that one of the walls did not extend all the way to the roof. It was easy to make repeated trips over the wall into the warehouse and remove merchandise through the false ceiling.

Opportunities for Loss

The presence of janitorial or maintenance employees during off hours increases the likelihood of company loss. This is not always intentional on the part of the employee. Loss can result, for example, if the employee fails to lock the entry door after coming into the building. Three electric typewriters were stolen from a building in St. Louis because of such a failure. A burglar can also gain access by loitering near the entryway and forcing the janitor to let him in.

In other cases the employees are directly responsible, and they can be quite ingenious. An unscrupulous janitor may not only carry out company merchandise but he may also make long distance telephone calls if the switchboard is unsecured, or he may use the company postage meter for his personal correspondence or packages.

In Los Angeles, a janitorial employee realized that he might be observed if he carried merchandise through the front door, and all other entries were securely locked. There was a great deal of attractive merchandise in the building, so he wrapped the items he wanted to look like packages ready for pickup in the shipping department, put his brother-in-law's name and address on a company label, and mixed his packages with others awaiting shipment. Thus he utilized the company's own shipping facilities to commit thefts.

A wholesaler of electronic components in the midwest installed an alarm system to protect his warehouse and office building. He then gave the janitor a key to the building and a card pass so that he could call in to the alarm company whenever he wanted to enter. This wholesaler followed good security precautions with his own office and warehouse employees; for example, he restricted sales personnel from access to merchandise bins because some small components were valued in excess of $100 per unit, and a man could carry a hundred of these in a single pocket without becoming too noticeable.

When it was discovered that there was a considerable shortage in warehouse inventory and an investigation was made, it was found that the janitor had been "stealing to order" by part number. An outside company had been giving him about one tenth of the value of the components he carried out on a regular basis.

In another instance, a three-man floor-waxing crew used a key to gain entry to an office at about 6:00 P.M. The company office at this location was ordinarily closed at 5:30 P.M., and the waxing crew was allowed to set its own schedule. On the day in question, two of the company officials had remained late to supervise some loading in the warehouse at the rear of the building. They had taken the precaution of locking the doors to the office that entered on the street but had not yet locked the office safe. One of the members of the crew, realizing that the executives did not know the crew was in the building, removed several thousand dollars from the office safe. The crew then left the building and returned to complete the waxing job two hours later, after the executives had locked the safe and departed.

When the shortage was discovered the following morning, the facts known to company officials indicated that the office cashier had carelessly lost company funds or was guilty of embezzlement. Suspicion continued to focus on this employee until a company security representative methodically traced the possession and usage of the office door keys.

There are other possibilities for loss from unsupervised employees. A janitor who has almost unlimited access to company buildings and facilities may be in a position to perform industrial espionage for a competing business. At least he may be bribed to permit entry by an outside industrial spy.

Janitorial employees should not even be allowed to take out company trash without supervision. During a single night shift an unsupervised janitor in New York City recently removed 30 electric typewriters from a large office building. The machines were secreted inside huge trash barrels which were taken down a service elevator and temporarily concealed inside refuse dumpsters until an accomplice placed them in a truck.

Janitorial and maintenance employees also have been known to break into company vending machine money boxes and force an exterior door or window to give the appearance of an outside burglary. In one case of this kind, a janitor chiseled through the bottom of the company money safe after tipping it over. He then smashed the lock on the front door of the building and set the office on fire. An effective automatic sprinkler system put out the blaze, but considerable loss was sustained from fire and water damage. In the investigation that followed, the janitor was unable to explain away the fact that his fingerprints were found in the interior of the safe drawer from which money had been removed. He eventually pleaded guilty to theft and was convicted.

Utilizing Temporary Employees

It has been the experience of a number of companies that temporary employees assigned to work with valuable merchandise are far more likely to perpetrate thefts than are permanent workers. Temporary employees generally feel that they have little to lose by engaging in misconduct, and they are often drifters who are unable to face up to any type of regular responsibility.

Some companies that warehouse and ship merchandise of considerable value must use temporary warehousemen during rush periods. It has been found helpful to assign a regular employee to work with each temporary worker and to accompany him in all his duties.

Some companies have an advance understanding with nonpermanent employees that they will be subjected to search at the time of departure. It is seldom necessary to go through such a procedure if regular workers have been assigned to work with them. There are undoubtedly some who would regard a search of this kind as somewhat degrading, but, as noted above, there is nothing legally objectionable to such a procedure if it has been agreed upon in advance. The search here would be a condition to accepting employment. In any event, it is an effective control.

Construction Workers on the Premises

Some businesses have experienced serious losses from failure to control the entry and departure of construction workers making alterations or additions to structures or facilities. One approach to this problem is to require the contractor to give written permission for an inspection of his trucks or departing delivery vehicles.

If supplies or construction materials are taken out on the contractor's trucks, it is often difficult for guards to determine whether the contractor's employees are removing materials that were paid for by the firm. A written pass system listing the merchandise on the departing truck has been found helpful in situations of this kind.

Management's Responsibility to Protect against Loss

Security control is a function of management, which is responsible for maintaining control of property and ensuring the safety of employees. Management or supervisory carelessness can have costly consequences for the firm.

Controls over door keys entrusted to janitorial or maintenance crews are often inadequate. Keys of this kind are frequently used on a weekly or biweekly basis. When not actually in use, the keys may hang on a hook where they are readily available to anyone in the janitorial service. It is recommended that these keys be retained in a securely locked place, under the sole control of the manager or supervisor. Each key may also be kept in an envelope with a secure seal or signature over the flap, and the envelopes should be kept under lock and key.

Company officials or supervisors may go to great pains to make certain that company funds are secured at the same time they disregard commonsense procedures that would keep those funds intact. Not only must management protect money and other assets, it must also protect access methods that might make funds available to unauthorized individuals.

To illustrate, a substantial amount was found to be missing from the safe of a New Orleans concern. Two supervisors were positive that the safe had been locked and tested after the money was placed in the interior compartment. Subsequent investigation disclosed that the safe combination had been written out on the desk calendar of one of these supervisors and recorded on a slip of paper kept under the desk blotter of the second supervisor. The combination would therefore have been available to any one of about 50 janitorial or maintenance employees who worked unsupervised at night.

17

Hiring Practices

A PARADOX has emerged in postindustrial society. While technology and scientific advances have made it possible to expand the efficiency and output of machinery, the problem of motivating people to achieve production goals has become more complex. Staffing is one of the most critical of management functions today. It must cope with the apparent contradiction of having to impose more discipline to counteract growing losses at the same time it places more trust in employees' capacity for self-control.

A reassessment of hiring practices is in order. Employers are experiencing faster turnover than ever before, with the current trend being for employees to move on within the first few months at a job. Stability was at one time more prevalent. Organizations are hurt in at least two ways when short-term employees quit or are fired—through the added burden on employees who must meet production quotas and through a general lowering of morale. Both lessen worker effectiveness. Otherwise dormant questions about whether there are greener pastures elsewhere are revitalized when a colleague at the next desk or in the adjacent shop leaves. The drain on output can be considerable when a

164

few loyal workers have to hold down their own jobs and temporarily fill in on others until new help can be found. The inexperience of the substitutes handling unfamiliar tasks leads to increased accidents, slowdowns, more wear on tools and equipment, more supervision being required, and a higher incidence of scrap. These workers may question why management could not have hired someone in the first place who would have stayed on longer.

Retaining dishonest employees who should have been eliminated from the employment eligibility list before being given jobs is also a serious blow to the morale of other workers. Management loses respect when this type of individual is neither fired nor corrected immediately. Simply put, honest employees should be recruited in the first place.

An increase in absence is a good indicator of employees who are about to leave their current jobs. The practice of declaring a position vacant after an unexplained absence of more than three days was noted in Chapter 15. Losses directly attributable to absences cost American businesses approximately $10 billion each year.[1]

Each firm can determine the extent of its symptoms of poor hiring techniques by working up some simple ratios. On an annual basis for current and past years, the total number of grievances can be divided by the total number of budgeted positions. The total number of terminations (or differing types of terminations) can be divided by the same denominator. If these ratios for individual departments or an entire enterprise are becoming larger every year, a reexamination of hiring practices is clearly in order.

Management Often Draws a Blank on the Application Blank

The employment application form is usually a new worker's first contact with the firm. Here the company gets to look him

[1] Raymond Dreyfack, *How to Control Absenteeism* (Chicago: Dartnell Corp., 1972), p. 3.

over, to measure his caliber. This same form is also the key to how the new worker will eventually perceive the company, the supervisors, and the job. A poorly designed, crowded form indicates that the personnel department does not want extensive answers, so meaningful answers will not be given.

A job seeker faced with a form that provides a miniscule place for stating why he or she left a previous employer often responds with "I quit." This is truthful, but it tells nothing of the reason for leaving. Another reason why adequate room should be provided on application blanks for comprehensive answers is that otherwise job seekers may decide that their backgrounds will not be thoroughly checked, and if they are hired they will not be supervised closely. A climate of employee ennui can thus be fostered even before workers are hired.

Every attempt should be made by the personnel representative and on the application form to stress that full, clearly worded answers are expected. Shallow, confusing replies will be given little attention when all applications are screened together. A lined sheet can be attached to existing forms for answers to questions the applicant wishes to clarify.

Question about hobbies and diversions away from the job can give a more rounded picture of the applicant. These interests can be critical in determining whether a person can fit into a situation where teamwork or close trust is required.

Detailed questions about previous employment, financial stability, and family status are obvious methods of precluding thieves or malcontents. But it is only worthwhile to ask these questions if the answers are going to be verified. The importance of providing accurate, truthful references should be stressed. This can be facilitated by making available a complete collection of phone books and street address maps of the general area for job seekers to consult in the personnel office. The easier it is for the applicant to answer, the more thorough the answers elicited will be, and the easier it will be do do background checks.

It is good practice to conclude the form with a phrase for the applicant to sign agreeing that if the facts he or she states do not check out (except in minor areas where an honest mistake could be made), employment will be immediately ended, with no recourse to the employee.

In an actual situation an applicant for a security guard position falsified his application record by stating that he had no prior felony convictions. A short time after the guard took up duties at his new place of employment, it was learned that he had previously been convicted. He was discharged for falsification of the employment record, and then filed a claim for unemployment compensation benefits.

When this matter came to issue the court held that the guard was not eligible for unemployment compensation pay. It was pointed out that his statement was basic to his employment as a guard. The company was justified in discharging him and in opposing his request for unemployment compensation.[2]

In this case the court seemed to attach some significance to the fact that a satisfactory arrest record was a basic requirement for a security guard's position. The courts have consistently held, however, that falsification of an application is sufficient justification for discharge if the employing firm would not have hired the individual had the true facts been known.

For a number of years some U.S. firms have declined to hire job applicants with arrest records. These rejected applicants have included persons who were arrested on several occasions but may never have been convicted. This hiring policy has been followed because these firms were convinced that people who are frequently

---

[2] *Roundtree* v. *Board of Review*, 281 NE 2d 360.

in trouble with the law are not likely to have the stability that makes for dependable, honest employees.

The Civil Rights Act of 1964 prohibits outright discrimination because of race, color, sex, religion, or national origin. In addition, it forbids hiring practices that are fair in form but actually turn out to be discriminatory in operation. If an employment procedure operates to exclude any minority group, the company must be able to prove that this exclusion is definitely necessary to the performance of the job in question.

The U.S. Equal Employment Opportunity Commission (EEOC) has taken the position that Negroes are arrested far more frequently than white individuals, and that this frequency of arrest is a condition under which Negroes live in some areas. The position of the commission is therefore that an arrest without a conviction should not be held against a job applicant. The commission also assumes the position that persons arrested but not convicted should not be expected to perform less efficiently or less honestly than other employees. This seems to run contrary to the old adage that "where there is smoke there is fire," but it does give applicants the benefit of the doubt.

The EEOC has also taken the position that an employer violates Title VII of the Civil Rights Act of 1964 if he rejects applicants based upon adverse information from former employers without first giving the applicant an opportunity to rebut the unfavorable information.

The federal courts have supported these positions taken by the EEOC. Consequently, job application forms should not contain a question as to how many times an applicant has been arrested. The federal courts, however, have distinguished between arrests and convictions on the application form. If the employer is able to show that the job position is a very sensitive one with respect to honesty, then he may refuse to hire an ex-convict. For example, a hotel could refuse to hire one as a bellman who would have access to guests' valuable luggage. On the other hand, the hotel could not refuse to hire him for a "nonsensitive" position.

To avoid charges of discrimination, it is suggested that portions of application forms which inquire as to applicant's ethnic group and sex should be deleted.

Unless height and weight information has a definite relationship to occupational qualifications, it is also suggested that requests for this information be eliminated. This is because height and weight norms for some minority groups are generally different from those for the average applicant. Unless a definite purpose is served by requiring this information, it could be considered as having a possible discriminatory effect.

It is also suggested that marital status information be deleted from application forms. Questions pertaining to the number of an applicant's children may also be objectionable. If a female has children and is refused a job, she could maintain that the employer discriminated against her because of the fear that excessive absences would be required to care for them. If she is married, she could claim that she was discriminated against because she is more likely to miss work because of pregnancy.

There seems to be no reason to eliminate questions as to whether the applicant has ever worked for the company previously. Some feel that all questions should be removed that relate to the ownership of a car, home, or to the employment of the spouse. The argument here is that questions of this kind cannot be answered in the affirmative by minority groups, and they are therefore discriminatory. It is suggested, however, that a definite effort be made by the personnel interviewer to explore any matter verbally that might indicate the applicant's potential for reliability.

If a minority applicant has information in his background that reflects unfavorably on his suitability, it is recommended that sufficient time be allowed to enable him to explain this information if he desires to do so. A detailed log of instances of this kind may be of value in proving to the EEOC that the company is attempting to comply fully with governmental requirements, while still trying to protect company assets.

Background Checking

When the personnel department thoroughly digs into an applicant's background, discrepancies between fact and items detailed on the application form are sometimes found. Often such detectivelike work reveals startling information that would otherwise go unnoticed or unknown. By going a little further to verify such items as job history and credit standing, a more comprehensive evaluation of the applicant can usually be obtained. The view put together from face-value information provided by personality tests, interviews, and unchallenged application forms is far shallower.

The main question to be resolved during the background check is whether the applicant is dependable and honest. Experience has shown that people who constantly change residences are ordinarily not very stable on the job. An applicant should be questioned directly on this point to determine if there are reasons for such frequent moves, other than that of trying to escape from collection agencies. A credit rating check to determine whether the applicant has had trouble paying his bills may indicate whether he will steal from the organization if given the chance.

Other characteristics of applicants can be brought to the surface by good background detail work. The greatest source of useful information is often former supervisors and employers. Because it is almost impossible to test or interview for accident-free employees, previous employers can be questioned about an applicant's safety record, for example. Former superiors and co-workers of applicants should be asked about anything that could potentially affect performance on the new job. A history of sickness, family problems, garnished pay checks, and other difficulties can indicate instability which can lead to disinterest, disloyalty, or dishonesty. An extraordinary amount of a supervisor's time can be devoted to directing and controlling problem employees who should not have been offered jobs in the first place.

The hiring company must take the lead in background checking, preferably by speaking face to face with former employers and associates, as opposed to using written or telephoned communications. Little unbiased information is obtained if the applicant is asked to bring his or her own letters of reference. Such testimony is at the control of the applicant, who can discard unfavorable references to past personal and work relationships.

Direct conversations with previous employers and associates are stressed because people often forget small yet important facts over time, and personal contact can help recall them. If distance, budget, or a considerable backlog of reference checking makes it necessary to depend on written inquiries, it is well to remember that people usually praise more generously when they write than when they speak. Putting observations and opinions down on paper often results in structured thought which does not promote candor, and questionnaires are often answered evasively. Asking a former associate or employer to compose an unstructured, general letter, however, will usually boil down to the standard response: "Mr. Blank was a good worker." This does not indicate the degree of "goodness" of Blank in relation to other workers or whether the former supervisor would rehire Mr. Blank if he had the opportunity. It says nothing that may contradict the reason Blank gave for leaving this particular job and provides no information on whether he got on with other workers, the true level of responsibility Blank attained there, or countless other (and sometimes hidden) items that are useful to know in staffing.

It is customary for many hiring firms to ask applicants whether it is all right for *current* employers to be contacted. The employee's reluctance to approve such discussions is not unusual, and his wishes should be respected, even at the risk of frustrating security-conscious personnel managers. Often a worker returns to his job after interviewing with another firm to find himself in hot water with management, which now views him as disloyal.

Complaints by employees who feel they are in dead-end jobs or that promotions are not coming fast enough for their abilities and ambitions should have been handled by present employers long before interviews with other prospective employers were contemplated. Management must have time to determine whether the employee is sincere about his desire for selfimprovement and expanded responsibilities. If free and open discussions have been entered into with present employers, workers can count on an honest appraisal of their performance when they use supervisors as references. Managements which avoid or discourage such discussion stand the chance of sacrificing a good employee by leaving him in the dark or terrorizing him, and they sometimes miss an opportunity to keep a loyal employee in the organization by lateral promotion.

Preemployment Testing

Aptitude and ability tests of applicants are used by many employers to obtain data on skills and to forecast probable performance on the job. Clerical skills, manual dexterity, and mechanical abilities can be tested by this means. Intelligence and mental ability tests are used to get a measure of intellectual or mental development as well as skills.

In addition to batteries of skills tests, there are standardized attitude tests which can be given to potential employees during screening. Such personality inventories and tests can be used to indicate potentially troublesome employees, although there has been little success in designing tests to flag the employee who will be dishonest.

Test scores can also be used for confirmation of dubious answers on the application form, especially when these answers indicate that an applicant may not fit into a closely knit operation with other workers. For example, an interviewer would question both the responses on the form and the validity of the tests if the form noted that a respondent was an active member of the Chamber of Commerce and regularly sang in a church choir (two clues that he gets along well in groups) while the test led to an interpretation that people annoyed him.

Such tests should serve only as back-up data on applicants and should not form the major criterion for eventual selection.

Interviewing

The preemployment interview between the applicant and the company representative is the appropriate time to resolve any discrepancies that may have been noted in the applicant's forms, tests, and background checks. Explanations provided in the interview may require further verification and can result in additional question-and-answer sessions with the applicant.

Job interviews should be carefully structured and planned, and if possible more than one interviewer should talk to the applicant. The tactic of using an interview panel of two or more interviewers has been successful. If an important question is not asked by one panelist, chances are good that it will be asked by another.

Ideally the interviewing panel would be composed of a personnel specialist, the head of the department in which the employee is to be placed or a line supervisor, and a representative of top management. The department head, who is ultimately responsible for staffing in his department, may not have the knowledge or skills about the mechanics of the vacant job that would give him the capability of asking applicants probing questions concerning their abilities in such a job. Therefore a line supervisor may be delegated the authority to do the interviewing and selecting, in which case it is more important for top management to join the interview panel. The manager is more likely to have had training and experience in dealing with people in the work environment and in judging potentially disloyal, dishonest, or disinterested individuals. If higher management does not sit on the interview panel, consideration should be given to including someone from the security staff.

In interviewing, it is wise to remember that some people are chronic complainers. If an applicant downgrades a previous employer, the possibility that he or she may become disloyal if hired should be considered. Of course, some complaints against previous employers are justified, but it is reasonable to try to imagine what this applicant might later say about the new organization which could cause employee unrest. Interviewers should also be wary of applicants who have quit other jobs without giving reasonable notice so a replacement could be hired. History could repeat itself.

Recruiting Employees from Competitors

When searching for a qualified employee to fill a particular position, a logical source is a similar organization which requires the same skills and abilities. The question of recruiting employees from competitors is in some ways an ethical matter.

The courts have always looked with disfavor on hiring practices where individual employees are pirated away from competitors for the purpose of injuring the competitor rather than to satisfy employment needs. In a case of this kind, one firm hired a key worker from a competitor, not for any real need but to cripple the managerial ability of the other firm. A New York court allowed damages to be collected for the loss of the valuable employee under circumstances of this kind.[3]

The Personnel Manual

The advantages to management of establishing and circulating precise rules for employee conduct have been pointed out in previous chapters. In many cases that have gone to arbitration or the courts, the decisions have been based on whether or not the employee was aware of a company rule about the matter in question.

The precise statement and wide circulation of rules also is of value to the employee. Fairly enforced, straightforward rules need not dampen employee morale, especially if the "why's" of the "do's" and "don'ts" are explained. If a new employee cannot understand the reason for an established rule, he or she may decide to disregard it.

The personnel manual can be an effective means of ensuring that all employees know and understand the rules. Individual copies presented to new employees help them feel a part of the organization as well as placing them on notice as to what is expected. However, it is often difficult to prove that an employee has actually read the handbook or is aware of its requirements, particularly if he was not provided with his own copy.

In one case, a newly employed credit man was informed at a verbal briefing that he would earn two weeks' vacation pay per year. Eventually he learned that a personnel policy manual was filed in the company office, but there was no indication that he had reviewed the material in this manual. After returning from vacation at the end of his first year of employment, he turned

---

[3] *Kaltmann* v. *Geiser,* 82 NYS 2d 155, 136 A2d 838.

in a resignation and gave two weeks' notice, stating that he had obtained a better paying position.

Management refused to pay the man for his vacation time, pointing out the printed rule in the company personnel manual to the effect that employees are not entitled to vacation with pay if they leave employment immediately after vacation. The employee insisted that he had never heard of this regulation and sued the company for his vacation pay.

This matter eventually reached an appellate court in Illinois, which held that "the vital issue is whether the employee knew of the policy in the booklet. He is not bound by it if he did not know of it or was not charged with knowledge of it." There was no showing by the company that the credit man had read the manual or had failed to read it after being ordered to do so, or that any official had ever brought the company rule to his attention. Accordingly, the employer was ordered to pay for the former worker's vacation time and legal expenses.[4]

Court decisions of this kind point out the importance to management taking appropriate steps to make certain that rule handbooks are read by employees. Labor arbitrators and judges seem to agree that posting rules or rule changes on a bulletin board is the most effective way of placing employees on notice. If the rule is prominently posted, courts and arbitrators will usually say that the employee should have known of it and is therefore bound by the requirements of the rule.

If a company handbook or manual is used, some firms have made a practice of chaining a copy of the book to a central bulletin board so that workers can examine it at their own convenience. This can nullify the argument that an employee is not bound by a specific rule because he failed to become aware of it.

Effective backing from the courts and labor arbitrators is also dependent on uniform application of company rules to all viola-

---

[4] *Olson* v. *Mall Tool Co.*, 104 NE 2d 665.

tors. Often a worker who has been discharged for a serious violation will claim that the rule should not be enforced against him because it has been overlooked in similar instances, or only token penalties have been imposed when other employees have committed the same violation. It is therefore advisable for management to make certain that not only are the rules made known to all employees but that the effectiveness of the rules is not diluted by failure to enforce them.

The advisability of making a personnel manual available for each employee cannot be overemphasized. In some instances when an employee asks to look at a departmental copy of a personnel manual, supervision begins to view the worker as contemplating what he or she can get away with in the bounds of published company policy. Often the employee is concerned only with minor personnel questions he or she does not want to bother the supervisor with: When does he qualify for vacation time? Who should he see to sign dependents up for group insurance? The manual can also be a major avenue for clarification in an employee's quest for self-improvement, providing information on qualifications for promotion or for employer-paid tuition for classes taken to stay current with technology and skills.

Changes and additions to the personnel manual and administrative regulations can be implemented by circulating them in draft form to line supervision and upwards for comments and review before they are finalized. This instills a sense of participatory management, and the feedback received often brings the front office in focus with on-the-job requirements.

Assuring Continuity for the Organization

The key factor in organizational effectiveness is instilling employees with positive attitudes toward the firm. Personnel specialists are trained to look for employees who not only have the requisite skills but whose attitudes are likely to be directed to team-work and interest in protecting the organization against internal and external damage. It is management's responsibility to explain to employees that losses hurt them directly, because they hamper the organization's ability to improve salary and fringe benefit structures.

Recruiting the new man for the loading dock or the new stenog-rapher for the typing pool should not be looked at as finding bodies to fill vacant positions. A more long-range view is that these new workers can become tomorrow's supervisors or man-agers. It is management's duty to hire people who are promotable so the company's future is assured.

To reach this end, it is well to look beyond any charisma the applicant may display in the interview and explore his or her past. While it is possible for a job seeker with a poor record to perform well in a new position, studies have shown that people usually behave as they have in the past. By starting with high quality, reliable people and motivating them to reach their best levels of accomplishment on the job, the organization can be almost guaranteed a continuing supply of loyal, competent employees.

Changes in Employees

Even though every effort is made to hire the best applicant for each position, employees can change. Circumstances can lead to character breakdowns which make employees no longer worthy of trust. Some are unable to resist the pressures of a money-in-flated society. Others become emotionally troubled and bring eco-nomic loss to the business and a burden to the community.

Until recently, employees' personal problems were not regarded as related to their work performance. An employee was supposed to leave his private emotions at the front gate in the morning and pick them up again as he left in the evening. Data accumulated in recent years, however, indicate that the employee's emotional state is directly related to his work performance. Accidents on the job, unintentional work slowdowns, embezzlement, or outright theft can be directly related to employee attitudes.

Increased costs for training employees have emphasized the need to identify personal problems and extend help to troubled employees before serious damage results. No one is expected to be, in fact, his brother's keeper, but certain signs are observable to supervisors and fellow employees as pressures build up. It is far better to counsel an employee privately about his personal problems than to find that he has attempted to solve his problem by stealing money or merchandise from the organization. Sometimes counseling can be implemented by assisting the employee to obtain a small personal loan. If a situation of this kind can be handled without creating employee resentment, management may be able to avert a breakdown in character and save company profits at the same time.

Employee Awareness and Loss Prevention Programs

Company loss prevention programs are dependent on trustworthy employees who are aware of their individual security responsibilities. The program can best be handled by a professional person who can command the respect of employees. Small-group meetings are effective to make employees aware of the program and emphasize each person's importance to its success.

Well-directed and provocative discussions can make employees more appreciative of the need for both physical and procedural security. The fact that confidential company information can leak out in conversation with relatives and friends can also be pointed out. A better understanding of security problems facing a company can make the employee more likely to accept the program.

The personnel portion of a loss prevention program should be directed to assuring three conditions:

1. That employees of personal integrity are hired in the first place.
2. That they continue to be trustworthy.
3. That they are aware of their individual responsibility to the firm.

In its efforts to assure security, management can cause personnel problems by overplaying its detective role. It is equally ineffective to assume an overly pious posture. If rules of control are clearly established, widely circulated, and reasonably audited, the program should be successful on its own merits. Management should not give up its own responsibility for a loss prevention program, but it should include employees as partners in it.

18

Proving Employee Misconduct

IN DEALING WITH dishonest, disloyal, or disinterested employees, it often is not enough for management to be convinced of their misconduct. It is also important to obtain proof of misconduct that will stand up if challenged by arbitration or a lawsuit following discharge. It may also be desirable for management to be able to refute a claim for unemployment compensation in the event an employee is terminated for cause.

Employee misconduct can be verified in a number of ways. Co-workers who are eyewitnesses to the questionable conduct will usually be truthful if interviewed in private and approached in the proper way. Generally, a co-worker will be less reluctant to furnish a written report if he has first admitted verbally that he observed the wrongdoing.

In some cases documentary proof may be available through company logs or quota records. Material of this kind can be protected by locking the documents in personnel or management files. Supervisory or custodial officials can identify each document by marking them with their initials and the date.

The guilty individual will sometimes admit his improper activities if confronted by a member of management who is well aquainted with the facts and the conclusions that can be drawn from them.

Closed circuit television cameras, concealed cameras, and voice recorders are sometimes used by management to record employee conversations or undercover operations. Misconduct can also be proved by making legal recordings of telephone conversations on company telephones. Undercover workers and polygraph tests are other widely used techniques in employee security operations. Corporate security may suggest some additional methods to prove some additional methods that may be utilized to prove employee wrongdoing, and these techniques should be considered provided the legality of the method is not in issue.

Closed Circuit TV

In a case involving the use of closed circuit TV, it became apparent to management that some employee in the mail-receiving room was rifling funds sent in for magazine subscriptions. In order to observe what was going on in the mail room, a closed circuit TV camera was installed. This brought an immediate complaint from the union at this company, which contended that installation of the camera was an invasion of employee privacy and asked that an arbitrator decide whether it should be removed.

The arbitrator ruled that the company was within its rights to install the TV camera. The reasoning was that the company could oversee employee work performance by installing a supervisor in the mail room on a full-time basis or by utilizing a mechanical device to afford somewhat similar supervision. The fact that the supervision was accomplished with a mechanical device did not interfere with employee rights.[1]

A number of union groups have conducted public campaigns

---

[1] In re *FMC Corporation, John Bean Division, Lansing Plant* (Lansing, Mich.) and *United Automobile, Aerospace and Agricultural Implement Workers of America, Local 724*, March 23, 1966, 46 LA 335.

to bar the use of closed circuit TV camera surveillance of employees, especially in warehouses and factories. The contention has generally been that the use of the closed circuit TV is a type of "spying" and an invasion of the human rights of workers.

It should be pointed out here that some firms have found that there may be considerable employee resentment to the use of TV cameras. If a decision is made to use this device, it is suggested that management point out to the rank-and-file workers that the cameras are installed on company property to control the firm's merchandise and are used as a tool to help management carry out its responsibilities. There is no more reason to resent the use of a closed circuit TV camera than to resent the installation of a dock lighting system to deter thefts from an open shipping area. It may be helpful to point out that the great majority of employees are considered to be trustworthy, and that the installation of cameras is not directed toward those who perform in a satisfactory manner. The object is to deter the isolated employee who might be tempted to steal.

Microphones and Videotape Cameras

The use of a microphone and videotape camera was considered justifiable in a case where a routine observation showed that articles from another department had been left in an area which was ordinarily used only for the storage of machinists' tools and clothing. A detailed examination of the area revealed property from three or four other departments.

Believing that someone in the machinists' room could be stealing, management authorized the installation of a microphone and videotape camera in the ceiling. The camera revealed the presence of two machinists and the microphone recorded conversations indicating that they were engaged in petty thefts and had knowledge of other similar acts. Both employees were discharged.

In a hearing subsequently sought by the two, the arbitrator held that the company could install and use any mechanical device on its own property to ascertain the nature of employee activities and to overhear conversations regarding theft. In effect, he held that the company could use any technical equipment so long as it was not illegal and was installed on company-owned property.[2]

Recording Phone Conversations

A great deal of publicity has recently been given to illegal telephone taps or hearing devices (bugs) that have been installed secretly. The basic legal objection to this equipment is that it has been put in place without the knowledge of the person who owns or controls the property, and he has no way of knowing that such installations have been made. It is another matter to record a telephone call on one's own telephone or to install a listening device in one's own property. As a general proposition, there is nothing illegal in recording a telephone call received by an individual on his own telephone, although the other party to the call had no knowledge of the recording.

Undercover Workers

Undercover workers are security agents who are placed in normal on-the-job situations to gain information management considers desirable. Such agents are seldom equipped with skeleton keys or sophisticated electronic equipment; usually they merely listen, observe, and report. Often they find answers to company questions that could not be obtained through regular business channels.

From an employee standpoint, it is human nature to resent "being spied upon," yet management's right to know what happens within the firm cannot be denied. The obligation to be in-

---

[2] In re *Disneyland* and *International Association of Machinists and Aerospace Workers, District Lodge 94; Local 1484,* April 20, 1972.

formed is distinct from a desire to pry into matters that have no connection with the business. Management need make no apology in its pursuit of company objectives.

The potential in using undercover workers to obtain information is almost unlimited. The practice can upgrade employee relations by revealing the condition of company morale, as well as finding such acts of misconduct as collusion with business competitors, falsification of company records, or production slowdowns.

Because the disclosure that an undercover operator is being used is likely to affect employee morale adversely, it is often preferable for the operation to be handled by a reputable outside industrial consultant or investigative firm.

If management makes a decision to utilize an undercover operator in the business, this decision should be kept completely confidential. Experience indicates that frequently a member of management will confide to another highly placed official that an undercover operator is to be used. It sometimes happens that the executive learning this information may actually be the culprit responsible for company losses. If not responsible himself, he may make disclosures to supervisors or employees who have no "need to know." When this happens, there is always a chance that the investigation may be compromised. Accordingly, complete discretion should be followed in using undercover agents.

Placing the secret operator on the job is a delicate operation which is less difficult if the firm has considerable employee turnover. Placement will also be easier if the personnel manager serves as safety and security director and can be taken into confidence. If security must be absolute, the undercover agent has to gain employment on his own ability. This may mean several potential agents must be interviewed before a suitable one is accepted as an employee.

The operator must be briefed on company operations and the information that is sought. Results often correspond with the amount of time spent in outlining company procedures, practices, and policies for the operator.

The undercover man must be willing to perform whatever work is necessary to hold the job. He cannot rely on his arrangement with management. If the agent has a better background than the job demands or does not have the basic skills needed, he will be under suspicion from the outset. He must neither overplay nor underplay the part.

The fewer pretensions he makes the better; it is difficult to alter one's identity, habits, and friends. There is always the danger that a chance encounter between the undercover employee and a former acquaintance may expose his real background. It may be necessary for the operator to spend some time with employees away from work in order to gain their confidence. An occasional glass of beer after hours can be helpful in employee disclosures once rapport has been established. If the undercover operator requests more and more "drinking money" to pay for his after-hours efforts, however, his value may become questionable.

In most situations, it takes time for the "new employee" to gain the confidence of his fellow workers. Anticipated results may not always be quickly forthcoming although an alert operator can usually observe significant facts within a reasonable time. An undercover man in a wholesale drug operation observed a trusted employee removing expensive drugs in pouchlike pockets sewn into the lining of his topcoat. In less than one month the agent discovered that the employee had stockpiled drugs worth $25,000 in the basement of his home.

Written reports from the undercover man are a requirement of the job. It is suggested that they be sent to the home of the cognizant member of management rather than to his office. Daily reports are almost always of more value than weekly ones, and details should be emphasized.

When the facts developed cannot be used without compromising or unmasking the secret operator, a decision must be made by management as to whether exposure is justified. It is to be anticipated that relations between management and employees could suffer when disclosures of this nature are made, and they should be avoided.

Value of the Undercover Operation

While an undercover program may be widely adaptable, it cannot be used successfully by management as a cure-all for failures to devise and implement controls. Firms that use undercover operators as the sole means of assuring security are avoiding their responsibility to prevent and control employee misconduct.

Use of the undercover employee should not be limited to detecting specific instances of employee misconduct. If the program is properly handled he can do more. He can take a constructive look at all the procedures used by management from a position inside the working force and can be a most effective means of determining employee attitudes and feelings.

In large concerns particularly, there is often a wide communications gap between workers and management. Executives and supervisors are therefore shut off from suggestions, signs of discontent, or legitimate complaints from rank-and-file workers.

If he is properly indoctrinated and briefed, the undercover man can furnish a wealth of information about company employment procedures, training and indoctrination, supervisory ability, and morale and can make an evaluation of management communications. In addition, management can use the undercover worker to determine whether the systems being used are adequate and how they can be implemented or improved.

The Polygraph as a Tool to Prove Misconduct

Neither courts nor arbitrators accept the results of a polygraph (lie detector) examination as evidence of criminal guilt or employee misconduct. This does not mean, however, that the polygraph is a useless investigative tool in obtaining evidence that can be presented in court. It is frequently helpful in inducing suspects to furnish a confession of guilt.

In one case an employee was caught removing merchandise from a warehouse and concealing it in his automobile. The employee readily admitted guilt but claimed this was the first time he had been involved. He pleaded for consideration and furnished management with the names of three other employees who had been removing merchandise from the warehouse.

These three employees, who appeared to be the major figures in the larceny ring, were interviewed and reluctantly agreed to take polygraph examinations. Results of all three tests indicated that the suspects were seriously involved and were withholding the truth. The three suspects were then discharged by management.

Since a labor union was involved, the three discharged employees appealed for reinstatement. The arbitrator ordered the three suspects reinstated, on the basis that there was insufficient evidence to prove theft. The basic problem of proof here arose out of the fact that the first employee failed to testify against the others. Although there was little doubt as to his responsibility, since he had been observed and had confessed, he still refused to implicate the others in court on the claim that he did not want to incriminate himself. Therefore there was not substantial evidence against the other employees. If the company had obtained a signed admission of guilt when the misconduct originally came to light, the outcome might have been different.

In another case, a cashier in a store reported a shortage of over $100 in her cash register when she returned from a coffee break. Management was suspicious of the cashier, who voluntarily agreed to take a polygraph examination. At the conclusion of the examination the cashier admitted that she had stolen the funds missing from her cash register and had previously engaged in other misconduct. As a result she was immediately discharged.

Subsequently, when the cashier complained to her labor union and asked for reinstatement, an arbitrator upheld the discharge. In this instance management was careful to explain that the discharge was based on the voluntary confession of guilt rather than on the basis of the polygraph test.

These two cases point out the way in which management should utilize the polygraph as an investigative tool and emphasize the fact that independent, outside evidence of this nature often results in a confession. If repeated independently to someone other than the polygraph examiner, the confession may stand on its own merit.

Generally, the courts have held that it is not necessary for the polygraph operator to advise the employee in advance of his rights. However, it should be noted that if the polygraph operator is a policeman who works for a business on a part-time basis, a confession will not be allowed by the courts unless the suspected employee was first given his rights.

Cash Register Irregularities

Retail businesses are often plagued by the failure of employees to record sales transactions on cash registers. What happens here is that the employee handling the register deliberately fails to record money tendered by a customer in payment for merchandise and, when unobserved, removes a like sum from the register and places it in his or her own pocket. In some instances the employee handling the register may fail to ring up the sale and put the money from the customer directly into his own pocket. In other situations, the employee removes the money from the register in advance, making up the shortage by failing to record an equal amount during the remainder of his shift.

The fact that the money accepted by the salesperson is placed in the cash drawer at the time of the purchase is immaterial. Likewise, it is not conclusive whether the employee's cash register balances out at the end of the day. When an employee manipulates the cash and the register entries, he can make his funds balance or come out short or over, as he chooses.

Use of a Shopping Service to Detect Failure to Record

If supervisors are unusually alert, they may notice instances of failure to record payments. Generally, however, the guilty employee merely waits until no one is around and then removes the money from the cash drawer. When registers are audited at irregular times, it may be found that a dishonest clerk has "built up" the cash but has yet to remove the funds which were not recorded. If the register is found to be short, it may be an indication that the employee has not had an opportunity to "make up" the amount of cash that was taken out at the beginning of the work shift.

The fact that a cash register is out of balance should not be taken as proof of employee dishonesty, however. The majority of retail clerks handling company funds are completely honest. No retail firm could stay in business very long if this were not true. There are times when anyone handling a cash register will make a human error. Some instances of failure to record are therefore good faith errors that involve a mental lapse on the part of the employee.

However, there will always be a few employees handling money who will be tempted to steal. To determine whether this is happening in a retail establishment, many stores utilize the services of a commercial shopping service. Members of a typical shopping service crew pose as regular customers and make purchases that involve ordinary transactions. While one investigator makes a purchase, the second member of the crew remains in a position to see whether the sales clerk rings up the transaction and places the cash in the register. Members of these teams or shopping crews seldom look like investigators or police officers, which hopefully will throw a dishonest sales clerk off guard.

In the usual transaction of this type, the shopping service supervisor informs the store manager or district supervisor by confidential telephone call that a failure to record was observed. At the close of the working day, the manager examines the detail tape from the cash register to substantiate the observations made by the shopping crew. This can usually be done if the crew is able to give the specific amounts of totals registered on the cash register immediately before and after the incident in question. In addition, the employee of the shopping crew will be able to supply a cash register slip number in most instances.

Management almost always prefers to prevent theft rather than to learn that an employee has failed to record a cash sale. Employers do not utilize the services of a professional shopping service for the satisfaction of detecting an employee in a wrongful act but to deter dishonesty by employee awareness that their registers may be checked in this manner.

Because there is always the chance that the employee made an honest error, the usual practice is to schedule a second shopping audit after an individual has been observed in a failure to record. If a second instance of this kind is observed, there is good reason to believe that the employee is a thief. The possibility that the employee could have been observed at the only two moments he made honest errors is extremely remote. Almost always the second situation occurred because the employee was looking for an opportunity to steal.

The usual procedure is for a representative of the shopping service to interview the employee after a second failure to record and to confront him with the evidence. In a high percentage of cases, employees who have been observed in this failure are frank to admit the theft in order to clear their consciences, often in spite of recommendations to the contrary from union representatives and friends. This is because many of these clerks have never been deeply involved in such dishonesty previously, and they are not customarily criminal.

Employers who do not like to admit that their employees are dishonest or who feel that taking action against an employee for failure to record condemns him on circumstantial evidence prefer to give a warning to the worker after a failure to record has been observed. A policy of this kind may be well intended but can cause a number of problems for management. In the first place, a warning to a thief could alert him to be more circumspect in future acts of dishonesty. In addition, it serves as notice to an employee that he may continue to fail to record until discovered and that upon discovery he will only be subjected to a warning. The manager who ignores a second instance of failure to record is deliberately choosing to overlook the facts.

Some employees will persist in claiming complete innocence. It is essential, of course, that the shopping service be reliable. All the facts must be accurately reported. If the shopping transaction cannot be completely observed, the employee should be given the benefit of doubt.

If the employee does not admit dishonesty after the second instance of failure to record, management may not be legally justified in discharging him for theft. He can, however, be released for "failure to follow established procedures in the handling of cash." If an employee has consistently demonstrated an inability to handle money, the company may be justified in firing him whether or not he is dishonest. The basis for this is incompetence. This approach, which does not label the discharged employee as a thief, has been consistently upheld by the courts and by arbitrators as a sufficient basis for discharge. The business simply cannot afford an employee who fails to follow procedures in safeguarding company money.

Taking Action against Employees When Theft Cannot Be Proved

While it is necessary to have proof of theft before dismissal on these grounds can be justified, other techniques can be used to take action when an employee's honesty comes to be questioned. One of the duties of a route supervisor for a newspaper consisted of collecting money from newsboys. On two separate occasions the supervisor reported that he had lost money bags containing cash collections. In the second incident, he maintained that he had gone into a telephone booth to make a call and overlooked the bag when he left the booth.

From all the circumstances, officials of the newspaper were skeptical that the incident had occurred as claimed. One incident of this kind would have been believable, but because this was the second occurrence management was convinced that the supervisor had taken the money. In addition, representatives of the police department had asked the supervisor to undergo a polygraph examination to make certain that the loss claim was well founded. The supervisor agreed to take the polygraph examination but did not keep his appointment.

Feeling that the supervisor was dishonest, management believed it inadvisable to allow him to remain on the job. Since there was no real evidence of theft, he was discharged for negligence and carelessness in handling company money. The decision to discharge the supervisor was upheld by the arbitrator when it was protested.

This case is typical of techniques that can be utilized by management when it has been determined that an employee is dispensable because of questions relating to his honesty that cannot be resolved. Even if the employee is basically honest, in cases like this he has demonstrated an inability to handle and retain money, which is undesirable from a company standpoint. It is likely that a discharge for theft in such circumstances would be upheld by a labor arbitrator where there is no disputing the fact that the employee exhibited the type of activity that made him suspect.

It is a mistake, however, for management to strain to utilize some such issue as an excuse for getting rid of an employee. In a case that illustrates this point, the manager of a group of optical stores believed that one of his employees was the only person who could have taken a sum of money missing from the safe. There was some reason for this belief, since there was no sign of forced entry and the facts indicated that the money had been taken by someone who knew the combination to the safe.

The suspected employee was asked to take a polygraph test voluntarily. The operator of the polygraph indicated that the results were inconclusive but some of the responses could be interpreted as reflecting guilt. Accordingly, the manager hired a private investigator to look into the activities of the suspect. Within a few days, the investigator reported that he had not been able to solve the problem of the missing money but he had learned that the suspect gave cash discounts to customers for eyeglasses and frames.

When the worker was discharged on the basis that he gave unauthorized discounts, he appealed to labor arbitration and requested to be reinstated. Management contended that the man knowingly gave discounts, although this was forbidden. The ex-employee argued that he was aware that the company had a rule against discounts but it had never enforced this rule, and numerous other employees gave special discounts to friends and relatives. He pointed out that the company had known of this practice for some time and had apparently condoned it since nothing was done to put a stop to the giving of discounts.

As a result of the arbitration hearing, the employee was ordered returned to his job. The arbitrator pointed out that there was little real evidence against the suspect and that the company had not taken serious action to enforce the rule against giving discounts. If the company had been serious about prohibiting discounts, then the rule should have been placed in writing, and employees should have been warned of the consequences of violation.

The obvious lesson from this case is that a person can be discharged if investigation of one suspected crime turns up evidence to indicate another violation. Management cannot seize on minor misconduct that is revealed by an investigation to discharge a person, however.

19

Terminating Employment

ONE WAY managers are judged is on their ability to select and recruit competent personnel. In the process of organizational development, however, it is equally important to know when to discharge an employee or let him seek work elsewhere. Termination of employment requires special managerial skills.

Whenever management is confronted with a submarginal or unsatisfactory worker it faces the sometimes painful decision of separating that individual from the work force. This may involve more than a temporary loss of earnings for the individual. The perception of employment held by most workers goes beyond regarding the job as the method by which they are fed and sheltered. Many social, nonfinancial rewards are also satisfied by employment, and individuals often incorporate their job roles into their personalities. The act of discharge, therefore, not only cuts the employee's financial resources, it also can deprive him of his social role or identity.

Except in cases of dismissal for dishonesty, however, termination can be a positive force for the employee. Keeping a poor

196

worker or one of little promise on the payroll may not be fair to either the individual's financial capabilities or his self-fulfillment. When a worker believes he is regarded poorly by management this evaluation not only disturbs him, it can diminish his potential. Management may discourage him when he seeks advancement within the organization, or it may find it necessary to dismiss him. Terminating such a worker can be to his own benefit in that he may realize he is not suited for this type of work or organization and will try another position or trade. His salary potential may be better and his relationship with management may be improved when he moves into another area of greater job suitability.

Management's Approach to Discharge

It is sometimes difficult for management to make the decision to discharge an employee. Some of the rationalizations for retaining an undesirable employee might go as follows:

1. Employees are hard to find. We could easily do worse.
2. We might be able to move him to a job where there is less exposure to loss or where he could do less damage.
3. I've got to look bad as a manager when I fire someone.
4. Training for a replacement costs too much.
5. In the final analysis, I hired him.
6. Firing him is bad for the morale of other employees.
7. Besides, I just don't have another worker who can do what he does.

Once these arguments have been laid to rest, management may find it has no choice but to let the employee go.

The company can face a costly lawsuit unless a dismissal for cause is carefully handled. This is true whether the employee is advised of the dismissal verbally or by letter. It is natural for an employee to exert pressure to learn the reason for his discharge, but management runs a risk in making allegations that cannot be proved.

In most situations the courts indicate that harm is sustained if publicity is given to unproven charges, either by letter or by word of mouth, but the employee has no basis for a lawsuit if he is dismissed in private and no publication of any kind is given to charges against him. Calling in a stenographer to take notes of the conversation or to dictate a letter of dismissal can lead the courts to maintain that publication has been given to the charges. It also is not advisable to have supervisors or co-workers present at the termination interview to serve as witnesses of employees' wrongdoing. This creates another situation that is regarded by the courts as publication of the charges.

The effect of such rulings is the practice of dismissing employees in private, without witnesses. If the employee insists on knowing the reason why he is being let go, management may advise him, but there is always the possibility of a lawsuit if these charges cannot be substantiated.

It is not necessary to keep the discharge of an employee secret from managers or supervisors who need to know what has happened and must plan to replace the employee, reassign his work load, or continue production without interruption. They must be advised in a confidential manner, however. There is no objection to one executive telling other executives about the reason for discharging an employee, provided the conversation takes place behind closed doors or out of the hearing of anyone else. If the conversation is held in the company cafeteria, however, it could be anticipated that the courts would regard this as unauthorized publication.[1]

To illustrate what can happen in a case of this kind, a former security guard at General Motors was awarded $24,000 because company officials told other security guards that the employee had

---

[1] *Bell* v. *Bank of Abbeville*, 44 SE 2d 328.

been discharged for unauthorized removal of company property. The facts were that the security guard had been observed leaving the plant with an automobile engine that was believed to belong to the company. The guard did not have the necessary pass for removal of this item from the premises. When the company verbally circulated the reason for this discharge, the released employee presented evidence which convinced the jury that the engine was not owned by General Motors, and the company had slandered an innocent employee. A verdict against the company followed.[2]

Records and Forms Regarding Terminations

It is good business practice to maintain a record of the causes for which employees have been discharged. It has been held by the courts, however, that such records must be factual and truthful. If erroneous facts are alleged and publication is given to them, the company will be liable for keeping a false record.[3]

In maintaining records regarding employee dismissal, care should be taken to keep the record under lock and key among confidential files. Rumors and unverified charges must not be cited as the reason for discharge. The cause should be listed only if the available facts will support the company's action in firing the employee.

The employer cannot be held liable for circulating the reason for discharge if this is required by law, however. In preparing forms regarding terminations required by local, state, or federal government, the employer does not need to exercise the same caution he must use in preparing his own personnel records. If there is a statutory requirement that the employer must fill out a form

---

[2] *Sias* v. *General Motors Corporation,* 127 NW 2d 357.

[3] *Hundley* v. *Louisville & N. R. Co.,* 48 SW 429; *Terry* v. *Tubbell,* 167 A 2d 919.

stating the cause of termination, he cannot be held legally responsible for giving publication to it.

For example, state law usually requires unemployment insurance forms to be filled out by the employer. Management is given protection in this case because it must reveal the record in order to comply with the law. If, however, it made some other use of the government form, such as distributing it in an employee bulletin, a lawsuit could be sustained against the company. The rule is that the firm is protected insofar as it is complying with requirements of the law.

It may also be necessary to state the reason for firing to union representatives if this is a requirement of the labor contract. In a case in which an employee was believed to have been falsifying time card records and to have stolen company goods, an investigation was followed by an interview with the company security agent. Thereafter the employee signed a written statement that he had cheated the company out of approximately $1,500 by falsifying work records. A copy of the admissions statement was mailed to the labor union, with a brief note stating that the employee had been fired because of the activities he had admitted in his signed statement.

The employee asked the union for assistance in reinstatement to his job, maintaining that during the interview he had been forced to remain in a locked room for several hours and that the signed statement had been obtained by threats and duress. He said that company employees had continued to hammer away at him until his resistance was broken.

When the union representative requested management's version of the investigation, he was advised that the interrogation had been completely voluntary and that the employee had been informed he could obtain a lawyer or union representative if he so desired. It was also pointed out that the security man identified himself as a company employee, and not a police officer, and that the employee was free to leave at any time. Management stated that the confession was freely given, and coffee breaks had been taken in the cafeteria during the questioning.

After looking into the facts, the union representative declined to ask for reinstatement of the employee. However, the ex-employee obtained an attorney and filed a lawsuit against the company maintaining that the employer had circulated a coerced, false confession by mailing a copy of it to the union representative.

The suit was dismissed by the Supreme Court of Kansas, which pointed out that there was a contract between the labor union and the employer which required the company to make a report of all disciplinary action taken against an employee who was a member of the union. It was held that the company apparently had acted in good faith and had not deliberately or maliciously sent out a copy of a false document. The court also noted that the statement had been given only to the employee's labor union and that no general publication of the confession had been made.[4]

Discharge for Off-Duty Misconduct

While management's right to discharge an employee for serious misconduct on the job is undisputed, normally the off-duty activities of an individual are of no concern to the company for which he works. There are exceptions when the employee's improper actions directly affect the company or indicate that he has serious emotional or criminal traits that will influence his job responsibilities.

In one recent case, a gas company installer called his supervisor to report that he had been injured in a "little scrape" and was unable to report for work. Over a period of ten years the installer had compiled an excellent work record, but management thought

---

[4] *Munsell* v. *Ideal Food Stores,* 494 P 2d 1063.

the facts should be looked into, and it came to light that the worker had been stabbed by a prostitute in a dispute over a bottle of whiskey. Investigation by the company security department also revealed that the employee had been arrested 16 times in the past six years—for child abandonment, disturbing the peace, assault, frequenting houses of prostitution, and traffic violations. Acquaintances admitted that he was frequently intoxicated and spent most of his free time in neighborhood taverns with known criminals and prostitutes.

As a result of these disclosures, the gas company discharged the installer. A union representative then filed a grievance in his behalf, demanding reinstatement. The union official noted that the installer had maintained an excellent work record over a number of years.

When the matter came to arbitration, the company pointed out that the installer was regularly sent into the homes of customers. Company policy had always required discharge for conduct that was "dishonest, dangerous, violent, or antisocial." Accordingly, the company claimed that the installer's activities and associates branded him as unfit to be sent into the homes of trusting and unprotected customers. The arbitrator who heard this dispute declined to reinstate the installer, agreeing that the employee had demonstrated a moral unfitness to be sent into customer's homes.

Cases of this kind indicate that some jobs carry social responsibilities which transcend the time and place of employment. The test seems to be whether the nature of the job requires the employee to maintain a degree of integrity that would make him acceptable for contacts with the general public. If the employee's duties kept him out of contact with the public, he would not be held to such exacting standards of conduct in his off-duty hours.

In a somewhat similar case, a long-time hospital employee was arrested for shoplifting. The amount involved in the crime was small, and the employee made restitution to the store. The case was given publicity in the local newspaper, however, and the employee was discharged when the news account was read by the hospital supervisor. Maintaining that her activities away from the hospital were not her employer's concern, the discharged employee appealed this decision through her labor union. When the matter came up for arbitration, the dismissal was sustained.

In support of its position, the hospital pointed out that the employee's job gave her access to watches, rings, and other valuable personal items owned by helpless patients in the institution, and a hospital should not be required to keep a thief in its service, even though she may have been completely honest at her place of employment. It maintained that the dismissal was proper, since it could be expected that the thief would steal in the hospital as well as in a retail store.

Discharge is normally upheld if off-duty problems render the employee unfit to perform properly on the job. In another case, an armed plant guard was fired for repeated drinking while off duty. The facts indicated that the guard had never come to work while intoxicated, but there was abundant evidence to show that off-the-job drinking had influenced his ability to perform his job. The guard had been repeatedly counseled to discontinue drinking but had refused to do so. With one minor exception, he had never been disciplined for any improper activity on the job. But the man's physical condition had deteriorated to the point where he could not be constantly alert, and he thus lacked the ability to afford physical protection to company employees. The termination was upheld by arbitration.

There are other situations which are exceptions to the general rule that an employee's personal life is his own. A discharge is usually justified if the employee engages in conduct that is so reprehensible that fellow employees refuse to work with him. Courts and arbitrators also generally uphold discharge for personal conduct that serves to aid the interests of competitors or misconduct of a nature that seriously injures the company's public image or reputation.

Keeping Lines of Communication Open

Fairness and awareness are the watchwords in skillful handling of discharge. Communications must be kept open between management and employees. Rules must be written so they can be understood by rank-and-file workers and provide no cause for confusion. If it is necessary to take disciplinary action, the company rule and the infraction should be clearly spelled out to the offender and a written record retained in the employee's personnel file.

Consistency in the enforcement of rules is essential. It can happen that one employee is discharged while another who commits the same offense is merely suspended without pay or reprimanded. The full facts of instances of this kind should be retained, as it may be necessary to prove that the worker who was dismissed had received numerous warnings, while the other had erred only the one time.

Ethics of the Departing Employee

The experience that an individual gains while at work is his alone. He can draw on it for background on another job and use it to make decisions and evaluations. He may also use his former contacts and continue most relations with acquaintances. But the fruits of an individual's labor—the compilation of materials he makes on the job—belong to his employer. Memos, reports, sales schedules and projections, blueprints, trade summaries, and customer lists assembled during the course of business are not the property of the employee who gathers them. They are collected for the use and benefit of the company, on company time.

Nevertheless, these papers and records give an individual a background for his job, and modern business has a great deal of dependence on paperwork. In moving on to another job, employees often have a need for material that has been found useful in handling similar work. It is an ethical consideration as to what paperwork a former employee should be permitted to take with him to his new place of employment.

A person who leaves one firm may go to its competitor in the future. Any firm would be at a disadvantage if everyone who left were allowed to carry off documents or information at will. It must also be recognized that in many businesses it is customary to raid competitors to hire talented employees who have considerable knowledge about the companies they work for. Recruiting of this kind is a part of the free enterprise system. Some workers are hired from competitors because of their demonstrated ability and willingness to work, but others are undoubtedly hired away because they are a valuable source of competitive information.

Courts and arbitrators are in general agreement that an employee cannot neglect his current job while preparing to accept another. He cannot decline to perform his assigned duties, such as taking orders, and he cannot solicit business from his regular customers in anticipation of a new venture he intends to undertake in the future. An employee is fully justified in looking for a new job or in planning to set up his own business without informing his current employer of his plans. If he has regular working hours, however, he cannot take action of this nature while on company time.

There is nothing to prevent an employee from advising current customers of his intention to leave the company and set up a competitive business. He can, for example, order equipment, hire employees, and rent a building for his new concern while still being paid by his present employer. But he cannot take any such steps to set up the firm on his current employer's time.

Confidentiality of Customer Lists

An issue frequently brought before the courts concerns the right of an employee to appropriate company lists of customers or confidential information about them. In one case a local sales representative compiled a list of 500 of his customers from telephone books and other public sources. He then sent out a form letter to all of his customers on the list informing them that he was leaving to organize his own firm and assuring them that he would pay close attention to their future needs and would be glad to serve them. Eleven days after this form letter was mailed and two weeks after giving his employer notice, the sales representative left and set up his own firm.

The sales representative's former employer went into court and asked for an injunction on the basis that the former employee had taken confidential customer lists. The court rejected the request for an injunction, pointing out that the list of customers was not confidential but had been readily compiled from telephone directories and other public lists. The court also upheld the sales representative's right to send out a circular letter before the time he left his old employer.

The decision in this case was on the basis that the customer list was not confidential but had been gathered from public information such as telephone and city directories. In another case, a sales representative who had worked for a firm for a number of years went into business on his own and retained copies of confidential customer lists and data on customers which had been gathered by his employer. He had been furnished keys to locked files containing confidential lists of suppliers, and company customers and specific information as to the buying habits of each customer. Some of this confidential customer information was maintained in code. When a lawsuit was brought against this sales representative by his old firm, the court found against the representative. He was required to surrender the confidential material and to desist from utilizing the customer lists and information that had belonged to his former employer.

The significant difference between these two cases is that in the latter dispute the company went out of its way to treat the customer information as confidential by retaining it under lock and key and keeping part of it in code. Generally, the courts are not inclined to protect customer lists when they can be compiled by checking directories, trade publications, telephone books, and other documents that are readily available to anyone. In addition, the courts will not be inclined to regard lists that can be compiled with only a minimum of effort as confidential. Another factor sometimes considered by the courts is whether the employee learns customer names and addresses during the course of his day-to-day work before he decides to seek out a new job.

The courts will usually protect customer lists as confidential if they are maintained in a secure place, preferably under lock and key, and if a code is used to protect vital information. If it is apparent that the company regards the information as confidential and takes any reasonable steps to safeguard it, the courts will be inclined to go along with the claim that the customer information is secret and belongs to the employer.

In another case the former employee took nothing in writing from the company but used his memory to draw up a new list of customers and addresses. Testimony in this case indicated that the employee had turned in all his customer lists and had taken nothing with him except a retentive memory. The court said that an ex-employee is entitled to draw on his memory for the names and addresses of customers and their peculiarities, indicating that this was a part of his business experience.

Rights to Company Records and Papers

It is written records, however, that are usually in dispute. In cases that have been contested in the courts, the decisions uniformly hold that if written information was gathered in the business and was necessary in handling the company's work, it belongs to the employer in the event that the person who compiled it goes to another company. It does not make any difference if the material is retained on the premises by the employee who collected it or if it is marked "personal" and is secured in his desk in the company offices.

The conclusion usually reached by the courts is that the records and books of a firm belong to the employer. If information was put together independently of the job, the courts will usually allow it to be taken. But statistical information, lists, data, or charts and other figures directly concerned with the performance of the job by an employee cannot be taken from the premises. If the data were compiled as a specific assignment or on instructions of the employer, they clearly belong to the employer.

Whenever information or property belonging to the employer is taken by an individual leaving the job, either openly or secretly, return can be forced by court order. In one case, an executive changing employers quit his job at the close of business on a Friday night. The following morning he returned with his son, gaining admittance with a key he had kept, and took away a boxful of diagrams, blueprints, production photographs, reports, and memos. There were no other employees in the office at the time, and the guards on duty did not question his appearance in the office. A short time later, the company discovered that confidential papers had been taken from his former desk. The ex-employee was questioned regarding this material and admitted taking the documents but maintained that they were personal items he had accumulated over a period of time.

The employer eventually went to court to ask for the return of company papers. The federal court that heard this matter ordered the immediate return of all documents, pointing out that statistical studies or documents compiled by the executive while employed by his old firm still belonged to that company. One of the factors the court apparently considered was that the ex-employee had "sneaked" back into the office on a Saturday when other executives were not around, this being the day after he had severed employment.

In another case, a research and development employee resigned for the alleged purposes of traveling and teaching at a university. He used the last two days on the job to gather his personal belongings, consisting of a considerable quantity of books, papers, and drawings, into boxes. Just before he left, the departing employee asked a company official if he wanted to inspect the material he was taking in order to clear it. The official declined to do so and signed a clearance slip giving permission for the boxes to be taken from the building.

Several months later it was discovered that the departing employee had carried away confidential information that enabled him to obtain the low bid on a contract for the production of a number of radar sets. The former employer then went into court and asked for monetary damages for removal of confidential data. The ex-employee felt that his act was justifiable because a company official had provided him with written clearance at the time he took out the questioned documents. In addition, he argued, all the information and documents taken had been worked out by himself alone, and he was merely using the fruits of his own labor.

When the matter came to trial in federal court, the judge ruled against the employee. The court noted that the company official who provided the package clearance slip never intended to allow the removal of secret company information. While he might have inspected the boxes taken by the departing employee, because of the latter's professional standing he would not be expected to do so.

While the decision here seems to be a just one, there is no

certainty that all courts would protect management in a situation of this kind. To make certain of legal protection, the company should restrict access to confidential information and prevent the removal of highly sensitive documents.

Stealing Customers

It frequently happens that an executive, sales manager, or supervisor will break off from an organization and go into business on his own. Often this break will not be made by an employee unless he feels he can take a considerable amount of the company business into his new organization. Sometimes this activity amounts to stealing the customers served by the first company.

The argument frequently made by the new firm and its attorney goes as follows: "Every business has a right to approach customers as it chooses, and we have exactly the same right to be in business as you do. You don't own these customers, you are simply trying to make a monopoly of them." The courts, however, are in agreement that a competitor does not have a right to solicit or induce the breach of a contract that is already in existence. The competitor, and everyone else, must respect existing customer contracts.

In a sales company it is not uncommon for sales contracts to disappear. Often they are stolen from the safe by a departing sales manager or supervisor. Therefore it is good practice to have copies made of all customer contracts so they can be introduced in court as evidence if the originals cannot be produced. At least, the original or one copy of customer contracts should be locked in a more secure place.

One of the problems that may arise here is that the customer may disclaim his signature on the contract or claim that his business was a partnership and his partner, "who must have signed the contract, died years ago." To establish that the contract is still in force, it may be desirable for the company's invoice to include a statement such as: "The merchandise furnished herewith is provided pursuant to a contract dated January 1, 1975 between us." Each time the customer receives merchandise, his representative will sign the invoice. This will serve to remind the customer that he does have a contract and will be convincing evidence in court if he should later maintain that he did not know about the contract.

If it should be determined that a former employee is endeavoring to solicit the business of a customer, a form letter can be sent to both the customer and the former employee advising that the customer is under a contract. If the competitor should succeed in taking the account, he then will be prevented from coming into court and claiming he was ignorant about any existing contract and had no way of knowing that this was someone else's customer.

When such precautions are taken, the courts can be expected to stand squarely behind the business with the contract. Not only can the presence of a contract be proved, but signed delivery receipts can be exhibited, as well as evidence that the competitor was put on notice. If the competitor persists in taking the customer, the courts will grant an injunction prohibiting this theft and providing the basis for a lawsuit for damages.

Inquiries Regarding Former Employees

The personnel job is not necessarily finished after the employee has left the firm. There is a continuing need to answer inquiries from other businesses regarding former workers. Most companies expect that other firms will honor requests for information regarding prospective employees and that this courtesy will be helpful in selecting suitable workers.

As a practical matter, every employee should be instructed to refrain from indicating any bad feelings in discussing a former worker. Quite often, individuals in any industry have a reasonable acquaintance with others in the same field. On occasions a member of management may become so embittered with an ex-employee that he indicates his firm will not do business with any company that hires him. The courts consistently say that every individual has a right to make a living and that a black list of this kind is sufficient grounds for a lawsuit, and damages can be sought from any person who endeavors to blacklist a former worker.

Anyone will have difficulty locating suitable employment unless references from former bosses can be obtained. There are a number of cases on file in which an individual has tried to force a former superior to provide him with a satisfactory letter of reference. A former steel worker once became infuriated when his employer filed a required form with the state employment bureau advising that the worker's services had been terminated because of unsatisfactory performance. After experiencing considerable hardship from his failure to locate a comparable job, the former employee filed a lawsuit against the company for which he had worked. The suit alleged that there was a custom in the steel industry requiring any company to provide a former worker with a letter of reference and requested damages for dismissal for "false reasons" and for failure to provide the worker with such a letter of reference.

This lawsuit was dismissed by the U.S. District Court, which pointed out that there was no way whereby an employer could be compelled to furnish a letter of reference to anyone unless there was a specific contractual understanding requiring it. The court added that no company is ever under any obligation to produce a letter of reference or to make a statement of any kind, written or oral, concerning the performance of a past employee. In addition, the federal judge pointed out that an employer can discharge an employee at will without being forced to supply a reason or to justify the discharge. This, of course, is in a situation where there is no union contract that provides arbitration or possible remedies against the company.

In most instances inquiries regarding a former employee are made by letter or by telephone. Some firms have a policy of replying to all inquiries of either type by telephone, placing nothing in writing. The only safe response of any kind that can be given is to be completely truthful. Insinuations or hints may never be repeated to the former employee, but if he should hear of false statements he may be legally justified in asking a court for damages.

Inquiries and replies should, of course, be retained in strictest confidence. All personnel employees in any business should respect this principle, but unfortunately this is not always the case. In one instance an individual asked for a reference from a former employer, and it was supplied. The current employer carelessly disclosed that the other organization had not given a favorable report on the individual. This resulted in a lawsuit in which the former company was forced to pay a considerable amount because of the inclusion of false information in the reference. This company then went into court and sued the current employer, pointing out that the information in question had been given in confidence and that this confidence had been violated. The court acted favorably on this claim and forced the current employer to pay damages for the careless disclosure.

To avoid such difficulties, an applicant should never be told why he was rejected. He can be informed that the firm has accepted applications from several individuals and has made a decision not to hire the applicant. He should not be told the identity of the person hired in his stead, and no justification need be given as to why another applicant was selected in preference.

20

Employee Development

THIS BOOK has examined aspects of how managers and supervisors can combat employee dishonesty, disloyalty, and disinterest, which can take the form of drug abuse, alcoholism, theft, insubordination, conflict of interest, absenteeism, and other problems on the job. One other area of insight is needed: Management should also consider itself as a potential cause for such loss-producing behavior.

If an employee can look to his supervisor and see that conscientious, loyal work has created only discontent in him, or if any of the actions of management are morally questionable, the tone for unrest has been set. It can easily trickle down from the top of the organization to all employees. Frequently workers place exaggerated emphasis on a supervisor's slightest word or act. When his gestures are even in a small way disintegrating to morale, the attitude can be: "If the boss is fed up, I can be too."

Why Do People Work?

Pay is not always the most important reason for wanting to hold down a job. Of course, individuals need funds for the basics

214

of life: food, clothing, and shelter. Beyond that, the worker often covets and appreciates the extra trappings that can be had with added dollars, perhaps a better car or a house with a swimming pool. Many socially oriented motivators for work are not reflected in the paycheck, however. Having one's name on the office door, being tested for future pay raises by being progressively assigned harder tasks, being able to say that one is an employee of X company when the community is aware that X company makes the best product on the market—such things are also of value to the employee. Perhaps the most important nonmenetary compensations for work appeal to basic self-interest: recognition for a job well done, having an extra day off that other employees do not receive, being assigned a competent staff so that tedious details can be avoided, or self-fulfillment in a job that is enjoyable and akin to one's hobbies.

Management's duty is to find the right combination of financial, status, and self-fulfillment rewards that will encourage high quality work and satisfied employees. Even rank-and-file workers whose wages limit their goals to paying for housing, clothing, and food can be motivated to do a better job by such rewards. Providing social stimulators can often enhance loyalty at little cost to the organization. Nevertheless, some old-school managers fear that if working conditions are improved too much, employees will become lax. Both ideas should be evaluated in setting up a compensation system.

Alleviating Boredom

Research and experience provide evidence of an increasing incidence of poorly motivated, frustrated, and unhappy workers, as well as a tendency for productivity to decline. A principal cause of these factors is that too many jobs are routine. Once the pattern of a particular task is learned, many work assignments become so dull that all concern for doing a good job disappears. Interest falls to a more basic level: how to survive another uneventful day. Some employers have taken positive steps to re-create interest, recognizing that everyone likes to feel that his or her job merits some regard from co-workers and outsiders.

An operations manager of two large departments in a southern California city government has instituted a Zero Defects awards program for workers who are selected by management for demonstrating outstanding skill, initiative, creativity, or quality. He notes that "We all hear about it whenever an employee gets chewed out, but no one finds out when a job is done well. This program gives such recognition for high performance." While there is no cash award associated with the program, each quarter the new Zero Defects winner is presented with an attractive certificate that is signed by the department manager, the city manager, and the mayor at a city council meeting. Pictures of the presentation are put in local newspapers, and the scroll is usually displayed at the winner's work station.

A recent strike at a General Motors plant was said to be caused by mounting pressure on workers to produce high quotas, coupled with the excessive dullness of the assembly line. Unfortunately for management, this particular plant operation, where Vegas were made, was designed as GM's pinnacle of efficiency.

Dullness may have been acceptable to the turn of the century worker, who was often an immigrant. Today a more educated and aware employee is manning the production line. Ceaseless repetition of the same task does not sit well with such a person. For this reason many organizations have sought ways to give workers more challenges, responsibilities, and freedom to act alone. Channels of communication are being opened so that employee difficulties, or evidence of exceptional performance, can get back to the higher echelons for action or comment.

American Telephone and Telegraph attacked monotony by

drastically redesigning jobs. This company was aware of employees' attitudes that machines were taking charge. As the market was demanding a more sophisticated product, it was possible to make line employees more than gauge watchers. Control was given back to the worker, whose self-esteem improved. Stop-gap measures such as team building and participatory management also have helped.

The New Breed of Employee

The new breed of employee with which management must now deal is represented by the liberated woman, the Vietnam-era veteran, and the recent college graduate. These types of employees are likely to respond to different motivators than their predecessors did. Often this worker is inaccurately stereotyped by management. To further complicate management's perceptions, the values or benefits desired by the new breed can come to be adopted by all workers.

One drive which can motivate recruits to management is their desire to start at the top. The education provided by many schools of business and public administration, which emphasizes executive simulation, organizational strategies, and decision making, could qualify many baccalaureate and masters holders for vice presidencies. All that is missing for obtaining such high positions is the experience that is earned by gluing the seat of one's trousers to a desk chair for a number of years. Perhaps industry is at fault for creating disenchantment in the recent graduate because it has perpetuated the myth that a degree guarantees management status. Some work experience programs have helped to dispel this misconception. In these programs universities and the business community get together to offer college credits, and some pay, to students holding down part-time trainee positions. At the end of the semester each student writes a synopsis of the practicalities he or she has observed, often stressing how the realities are in conflict with the textbooks. At very low cost to the training organization, management has been given the opportunity of selecting or rejecting future junior executives. Students can see if such an occupation is to their liking before devoting four years of college in pursuit of a career objective that might prove disappointing.

There are some misconceptions about young people entering the job market. One is that the new worker is not profit oriented but is concerned instead with corporate responsibilities to consumers and to the environment. Many 20-year-olds are not only aware of the necessity of profits, they are encouraged by the tendency of business to couple profits with social responsibilities. More publicity should be given to evidence of such concerns as demonstrated by firms.

It is natural for employees to be anxious about the fairness of the pay they receive. The worker who feels he is being paid less than another who contributes less than he does has an understandable complaint. When it is explained that seniority should be rewarded, the newer breed of worker can usually see the merits of long-time loyalty.

Changes of locale—as opposed to having only one work area—and increased physical activity are often required by the younger employee as means to counter boredom. Rotational training programs are often a good idea.

Perhaps the most important incentive for the new breed is his perception of the importance or usefulness of his job. It has been noted that employees always want to do useful work. When brass workers building ammunition cartridges in World War II were assigned to make lipstick holders after the war, their attitude went from positive to negative.[1] If there is a problem regarding how

---

[1] Lawrence Finley and Travis Pritchett, "Managing the New Breed of Employee," *Personnel Journal*, January 1973, p. 49.

workers view the necessity of their assignments, it may be good to maximize its importance so outsiders will place more value on the work being done.

Women in the Work Force

A conversation similar to the following is not unusual:

"Let me speak to one of the technicians. I'd like to discuss the XYZ project."

"You could talk to me. I'm familiar with that project."

"But you're a woman."

"I'm also a technician."

There are 33 million working women in the United States, comprising almost 40 percent of the nation's labor pool. Essentially, they work for the same reasons that men do.[2]

The potential for women employees to be dissatisfied with their jobs is tremendous. Relatively few women workers are given the same amount of on-the-job training and development that their male counterparts have received. Women are generally subject to tokenism similar to that accorded the minority races in the 1960s. Although they are hired, they are frequently skipped when promotions are made. This is particularly hard to justify because more women are receiving college degrees than ever before.

Federal legislation has begun to improve conditions for women in the areas of hiring and advancement. However, more should be done on the employer's initiative.

Recently, IBM Senior Vice President George S. Beitzel defined industry's biggest problem in the coming years as "a shortage of capable people at all levels of management." If this is true, corporate leaders can no longer ignore half of the population when they are looking for creative and executive talent.[3]

---

[2] M. Barbara Boyle, "Equal Opportunity for Women Is Smart Business," *Harvard Business Review*, May–June 1973, p. 86.

[3] Ibid., p. 87.

The Management of Mistakes

There is a conflict between the way talented employees are hired and the way they are promoted. Organizations prefer to staff themselves with innovators, but innovation involves experimentation, which inevitably results in some mistakes being made by the experimenter. Employees who make mistakes are usually not considered to be worthy of hiring or promotion. Thus the proper management of mistakes is a skill that should be developed so that subordinates with leadership qualities can be given jobs where this ability can be used rather than being confined to unchallenging niches. All too often, the only time an employee hears from his boss is when he has made an error. Training programs stress the avoidance of mistakes when they should be expanding the learner's available potential skills.[4]

It is often better for management to explore *why* the mistake was made instead of concentrating on reprimanding the mistake maker. Criticism will not always correct future mistakes, but discipline should be used when carelessness is involved. A worker's preoccupation with a personal problem which results in subgrade output cannot be straightened out by destructive supervisorial comments.

After the reason for the mistake has been identified, the next step is to set up an attitude of receptivity for change on the part of the mistake maker. This is not done by stressing that the supervisor is on top and the line worker will always be on the bottom if such mistakes continue. If the worker is shown the advantages he or she will obtain in personal terms from error-free work, the possibility of potential mistakes will be diminished. The fewer mistakes that are made, the higher the efficiency, and the less waste. Less waste means more profits and higher salaries for workers.

------

[4] C. R. Grindle, "The Management of Mistakes," *Nation's Business*, June 1972, p. 72. Copyright © 1972, Chamber of Commerce of the United States.

When supervisors discover errors in subordinates' work, it is sometimes possible to institute a learning process whereby the worker, after reflecting upon the mistake, can be counseled and asked for his advise on how similar errors can be avoided. This promotes employee growth. With managerial experience and guidance, the employee learns how to solve problems on his own and, simultaneously, how to stay within the constraints of good operating practices. The aim is to encourage foresight into all the alternatives that can follow from a certain action. What would happen if a contract were not fully studied before it was signed? What would happen if a file on an important client were misplaced?

Having an individual check his or her own work is also effective. It is sage advice that "If it looks wrong, it probably is wrong." Correcting one's own errors—especially the simpler, more glaring ones—can save the supervisor's time and build up the supervisor's confidence in the worker. The worker can also get a better understanding of the assignment when he digs into the subject deeper before seeking the supervisor's approval. In such a procedure, the subordinate does his or her own job development.

The use of common sense to avoid and correct mistakes is vital. An assignment may be completed in an unusual way which produces controversial results. Upon receipt of such a finished product, management will be tempted to point out the possible mistakes that have been made. It is wise to anticipate such disbelief, double check controversial areas, and present a straightforward explanation with the assignment when it is passed upward.

Flattery

A supervisor's misuse of flattery as an employee development tool, like inept handling of mistakes and management by fear, can result in lower morale and poor production. Some managers administer no discipline when things go wrong and are lavish with compliments when average output is attained. Such praise is usually detected as being false by workers. It is just as wrong for the supervisor not to commend an individual for a good job, while silently maintaining the attitude that the best is always expected.

Some individuals take praise well, but only when it is given in private. Others prefer to be honored in front of their colleagues. One administrator feels that retirement testimonial dinners should be given at midcareer instead of at the end. As it is now, such tributes tend to fire up the honoree positively for better performance . . . although he or she has already checked out of the organization.

Disillusionment

Whenever a worker's expectations of what the job holds for him do not meet with reality, chances for frustration or turnover are high. This often happens with employees who do not look into the duties and potential for advancement of a job before accepting it.

The best time to equate job expectation with reality is during the hiring process. One way to do this is by having the applicant talk to the individual he or she will be replacing. This makes it possible, for example, for a person interviewing for a journeyman's position to verify with the former journeyman how long it took him to become appointed to a foremen's job. The real duties that are often not included in the advertised job description can be discussed with a person who has had first-hand experience.

Other outfits have been successful in realistically describing jobs by itemizing in booklet form the number of hours that must be devoted to different tasks each week. Some candidates for work in this situation may read the booklet, say, "Oh! *This* is what this job involves," and voluntarily withdraw their application forms. This is better than wasting the employer's time and money by a recruit's halfheartedly entering into an expensive training program with the hope of growing to like the job.

Most employers do not purposely try to trick applicants with false expectations of what a job can *eventually* become by omitting descriptions of the hard work involved in obtaining such a position, but a few firms persist in this practice. One contemporary example of this is the company that advertises for management and consultant vacancies to be filled. Applicants who call for an appointment are not even given the name of the firm. At the interview which is given to many applicants at the same time, sales promotion for a specific line of products and appeals to the group and to the joiner instinct make it apparent that the position offered is that of salesman. Ordinarily, new people who sign on start as enthusiastic salesmen but quit with considerable malaise when the promised management jobs never open. The firm might have better success with pointedly advertising for a sales position in the first place.

Various manufacturers have been successful in disspelling misconceived expectations by giving applicants tours of the operational areas midway into the hiring process. While more candidates for employment abandoned the application procedure at this point once the tour was included, it was felt by management that an increased number of dedicated, realistic individuals were hired when this step was included than had previously been the case. Thus the elimination of surprises can be beneficial to both employer and employee.

Summary

Many employee-employer problems are the result of the growth of a successful organization: the boss is in charge of too many individuals to stay close to all of them. Such items as seniority are often misunderstood by workers and misused by managers.

The reason many workers today do not meet the performance standards of management is often because necessary skills are lacking. Management is at fault when an employee displays a wish to improve on such skills but is not shown the vehicle for doing so. Work measurements cause tension when there is no agreement between workers (who state attainable goals) and supervisors (who mouth requested goals from the executive suite). Line operators are out of touch with top management, and suggestions from below are occasionally not received, or if they are received and acted upon there is no report back to the subordinate who instituted the idea. For this reason in some organizations few innovations are passed forward from assembly and maintenance personnel—the very people who are closest to the problem areas.

Sometimes the system stands in the way of job development. Those at the top are reluctant to deviate from tradition, even for a logical reason, because tradition has maintained the organization and helped it grow.

As a step in avoiding these problems, the following checklist for managers and supervisors can be used to measure the extent to which professional growth of employees is being supported.

1. Do you do all you can to keep your employees informed about contemplated changes in equipment, procedures, and techniques? Do you explain the reasons for such changes and encourage acceptance?
2. Do you have meetings with your people to go over problems they may have and answer questions about policies, equipment, or procedures?
3. Do you have individual performance-review sessions with your employees to draw out their personal feelings, give constructive tips, and encourage their personal growth on the job?
4. Have you recently suggested courses, reading materials, or other

self-improvement devices to help them better their jobs skills and knowledge?

5. Are you well enough informed yourself about trends in your own area to give employees tips on what will be demanded of them in the months and years ahead?
6. Can you honestly say that most of your subordinates know more about their jobs and skills than they did six months ago?
7. Can you point to any individuals in your work group who would be up against it jobwise if certain mechanized changes were made?
8. If you answered "yes" to no. 7, can you establish a program to help that person or persons prepare for other types of work related to what they are now doing?[5]

The manager's primary job is to get things done through others. It is his or her duty to encourage employees' job development in order to alleviate problems of dishonesty, disloyalty, and disinterest.

[5] Raymond Dreyfack, *How to Control Absenteeism* (Chicago: Dartnell Corp., 1972), pp. 12–13.

INDEX

General Index

229

Control of employees entering or
leaving
confidential union business,
150–151
construction workers on the premises, 161–62
curtailing janitorial access, 157–58
discharge, 150
door keys, 159–60, 162
employee lockers, 155–56
employees who work unsupervised,
156–57
inspection of packages and briefcases, 149–51
opportunities for loss, 158–61
package passes (example), 153
postage meters, 158–59
rules, 154
search of contractor's vehicles,
161–62
search of temporary employees,
161
searches, 154–56
searches on government property,
151–52
shipping facilities, 159
telephones, 158–59
Controlling office supplies
attitudes toward pilferage, 83
benefits to workers from deterring
theft, 83
little value of items stolen, 82–83
Controls, poor record keeping, 135
Copying machines, 73–75
Corporate directors and conflict of
interest, 117–21
Credit cards, 75
Criminal offense for bribing a purchasing agent, 71
Customer lists, 206–7
Customer relations, 96

D

Dallas General Drivers, Warehousemen, and Helpers, 51
Damaged merchandise, 66–67
Determining whether prices paid are
excessive, 72

Discipline, 130
absenteeism, 146
dissimilar punishment for the same
offense, 99–100
does the punishment fit the crime?
98–100
records, 146
rest period, 143
Dishonest executives, 6–7
Dismissal, 130
absenteeism, 136–38
abusive language to management,
92–94
although acquitted in court for
theft, 61–62
as an advantage to the worker,
197
attempted theft is sufficient for,
62
boycotting company product, 97–98
employees who enjoy public trust,
201–3
expense account padding, 131–32
falsification of records, 131, 134–35
management's approach to, 197–99
off-duty misconduct, 201–4
overpayment of employees, 133–34
proof from microphones and
videotape, 183–84
refusal to permit search, 150–51
refusal to work, 94–95
secret from other managers, 198–99
social responsibility, 202–3
taking action when theft cannot
be proved, 193–95
theft, 59–60
unauthorized discounts, 193–95
witnesses to, 198
Disneyland, 183–84
Dreyfack, Raymond, 136, 165,
224–25
Drug abuse
amphetamines, 14–15, 23
barbiturates, 14–15
cocaine, 23
codeine, 14
cost to the organization, 12
detection, 15–16
"downers," 16

DATE DUE